THE MECKLENBURG DECLARATION OF INDEPENDENCE

MAY 20, 1775

AND LIVES OF ITS SIGNERS

THE MECKLENBURG
—NORTH CAROLINA—
DECLARATION *of*
INDEPENDENCE

MAY 20, 1775

and
Lives of Its Signers

George W. Graham, M.D.

HERITAGE BOOKS
2009

HERITAGE BOOKS
AN IMPRINT OF HERITAGE BOOKS, INC.

Books, CDs, and more—Worldwide

For our listing of thousands of titles see our website
at
www.HeritageBooks.com

A Facsimile Reprint
Published 2009 by
HERITAGE BOOKS, INC.
Publishing Division
100 Railroad Ave. #104
Westminster, Maryland 21157

Copyright © 1905 George W. Graham, M.D.

Index Copyright © 2000 Heritage Books, Inc.

— Publisher's Notice —
In reprints such as this, it is often not possible to remove blemishes from the original. We feel the contents of this book warrant its reissue despite these blemishes and hope you will agree and read it with pleasure.

International Standard Book Numbers
Paperbound: 978-0-7884-1564-7
Clothbound: 978-0-7884-8104-8

CONTENTS

	PAGE
Preface	5
The Mecklenburg Declaration of Independence	9
The Thirty-first Resolves	38

The Lives of the Signers and a Few Spectators:

Gen. Thomas Polk	84
Col. Abraham Alexander	100
Dr. Ephraim Brevard	103
Col. Adam Alexander	107
Gen. Robert Irwin	110
John McKnitt Alexander	111
Rev. Hezekiah Balch	114
Hezekiah Alexander	116
Capt. Zaccheus Wilson	117
Neil Morrison	120
Richard Barry	121
John Flennikin	122
William Graham	123
Matthew McClure	123
John Queary	124
Ezra Alexander	124
Waightstill Avery	125
Col. William Kennon	127
Col. James Harris	128
David Reese	129
Henry Downs	130
John Foard	131
Charles Alexander	132
Robert Harris, Sr	132
Maj. John Davidson	134
Col. Ezekiel Polk	136
Capt. James Jack	137
Rev. Francis Cummings, D. D.	139
Gen. Joseph Graham	140
Gen. George Graham	142

Appendix—Documents Cited in Preceding Address:

Martin's Preface	146
Pamphlet Issued by the Legislature of North Carolina, 1831.	151

PREFACE

This monograph upon the Mecklenburg Declaration of Independence was read before the Scotch-Irish Society of America at its meeting in Lexington, Virginia, on June 21, 1895, and is printed in Vol. VII of the transactions of that association. It has since been revised and enlarged and several separate editions issued in pamphlet. And, as the demand for the essay has exceeded the writer's expectations, it is now published in book form with a short biography of the signers of the declaration added.

The author will be found to differ with some advocates of the Mecklenburg Declaration, in that he acknowledges the verbal errors of the Davie copy of the resolutions, defines the position of the Thirty-first Resolves in the controversy, and shows why Martin's History of North Carolina is authentic, and therefore contains a correct account of the famous convention at Charlotte on May 19-20, 1775.

Since this address was first presented to the Scotch-Irish Society, a number of writers, usually newspaper contributors, have copied freely from it and displayed their productions in the press without either quotation marks or any acknowledgment whatever as to the source of their information.

The reader that desires to examine the authorities cited in this paper will find in the appendix a transcript of the Davie copy of the Mecklenburg Declaration, so much of the preface to Martin's History as is pertinent to our subject, and a copy of the pamphlet issued by the Legislature of North Carolina in 1831, containing Mr. Jefferson's letter to John Adams, and the testimony of spectators and delegates to the twentieth of May convention, as well as other interesting data germane to this question.

GEORGE W. GRAHAM, M. D.

Charlotte, N. C.
April, 1905.

THE MECKLENBURG DECLARATION OF INDEPENDENCE

MAY 20, 1775 *

Mr. President, Ladies and Gentlemen:

The subject of our address to-day is the Mecklenburg Declaration of Independence, a theme of deep interest to the Scotch-Irish fraternity, as the first men in America to cast off the British yoke were members of that brotherhood. The genuineness of this declaration has long been a subject of controversy among historians, because at the time of their writing all the proofs of its authenticity had not been gathered. During the past four years, we, aided by Professor Alexander Graham of Charlotte, North Carolina, have made a thorough investigation of this question, and now present to your honorable assembly the result of our research. It will be found to contain much new evidence that has never appeared in print, and, we think, will remove all doubt as to there having been a Declaration of Independence by the Scotch-Irish of Mecklenburg on May 19-20, 1775.

The history of the adoption of this declaration, its publication, and the subsequent controversy regarding it, runs as follows:

---

* See Preface.

"In the months of March and April, 1775, the leading men in the county of Mecklenburg held meetings to ascertain the sense of the people, and to confirm them in their opposition to the claims of Parliament to impose taxes and regulate the internal policy of the Colonies. At one of these meetings, when it was ascertained that the people were prepared to meet their wishes, it was agreed that Thomas Polk, then colonel commandant of the county, should issue an order directed to each captain of militia, requesting him to call a company meeting to elect two delegates from his company to meet in general committee at Charlotte on the 19th of May; giving to the delegates ample power to adopt such measures as to them should seem best calculated to promote the common cause of defending the rights of the Colony, and aiding their brethren in Massachusetts. Colonel Polk issued the order, and the delegates were elected. They met in Charlotte on the day appointed. The forms of their proceedings and the measures to be proposed had been previously agreed upon by the men at whose instance the committee were assembled. The Rev. Hezekiah Jones Balch, Dr. Ephraim Brevard, and William Kennon, Esq., an attorney at law, addressed the committee, and descanted on the causes which had led to the existing contest with the mother country, and the consequences which were to be apprehended unless the people should make a firm and energetic resistance to the right which Parliament asserted of taxing the Colonies and regulating their internal policy.

"On the day on which the committee met, the first intelligence of the action at Lexington, in Massachusetts, on the 19th of April, was received in Charlotte. This intelligence produced the most decisive effect. A large concourse of people had assembled to witness the proceedings of the committee. The speakers addressed their discourses as well to them as to the committee, and those who were not convinced by their reasoning were influenced by their feelings, and all cried out: 'Let us be independent! Let us declare our independence and defend it with our lives and fortunes!' A committee was appointed to draw up resolutions. This committee was composed of the men who had planned the whole proceedings, and who had already prepared the resolutions which it was intended should be submitted to the general committee. Doctor Ephraim Brevard had drawn up the resolutions some time before and now reported them with amendments as follows:

"'I. *Resolved,* That whosoever directly or indirectly abets, or in any way, form, or manner countenances the invasion of our rights, as attempted by the Parliament of Great Britain, is an enemy to his country, to America, and to the rights of man.

"'II. *Resolved,* That we, the citizens of Mecklenburg County, do hereby dissolve the political bonds which have connected us with the mother country, and absolve ourselves from all allegiance to the British crown, abjuring all political connection with a nation that has wantonly trampled on our rights and liberties and inhumanly shed innocent blood of Americans at Lexington.

" 'III. *Resolved,* That we do hereby declare ourselves a free and independent people; that we are, and of right ought to be, a sovereign and self-governing people under the power of God and the General Congress; to the maintenance of which independence we solemnly pledge to each other our mutual co-operation, our lives, our fortunes and our most sacred honor.

" 'IV. *Resolved,* That we hereby ordain and adopt as rules of conduct all and each of our former laws, and that the crown of Great Britain can not be considered hereafter as holding any rights, privileges, or immunities amongst us.

" 'V. *Resolved,* That all officers, both civil and military, in this county, be entitled to exercise the same powers and authorities as heretofore; that every member of this delegation shall henceforth be a civil officer and exercise the powers of a justice of the peace, issue process, hear and determine controversies according to law, preserve peace, union and harmony in the county, and use every exertion to spread the love of liberty and of country until a more general and better organized system of government be established.

" 'VI. *Resolved,* That a copy of these resolutions be transmitted by express to the President of the Continental Congress assembled in Philadelphia, to be laid before that body.'

"These resolutions were unanimously adopted and subscribed by the delegates. James Jack, then of Charlotte, but now residing in the State of Georgia, was engaged to be the bearer of the resolutions to the

President of Congress, and directed to deliver copies of them to the delegates in Congress from North Carolina. The President returned a polite answer to the address which accompanied the resolutions, in which he highly approved of the measures adopted by the delegates of Mecklenburg, but deemed the subject of the resolutions premature to be laid before Congress. Messrs. Caswell, Hooper and Hewes forwarded a joint letter, in which they complimented the people of Mecklenburg for their zeal in the common cause, and recommended to them the strict observance of good order; that the time would soon come when the whole continent would follow their example.

"On the day that the resolutions were adopted by the delegates in Charlotte, they were read aloud to the people who had assembled in the town, and proclaimed amidst the shouts and huzzas, as expressing the feelings and determination of all present. When Captain Jack reached Salisbury, on his way to Philadelphia, the general court was sitting and Mr. Kennon, an attorney at law, who had assisted in the proceedings of the delegates at Charlotte, was then in Salisbury. At the request of the judges, Mr. Kennon read the resolutions aloud in open court, to a large concourse of people; they were listened to with attention and approved by all present.

"The delegates at Charlotte being empowered to adopt such measures as in their opinion would best promote the common cause, established a variety of regulations for managing the concerns of the county. Courts of justice were held under the direction of the delegates. For some months these courts were held at Charlotte; but for the convenience of the people (for at that time Cabarrus formed part of Mecklenburg), two other places were selected, and the courts were held at each in rotation. The delegates appointed a committee of their body who were called 'a committee of safety, and they were empowered to examine all persons brought before them charged with being inimical to the common cause, and to send the military into the neighboring counties to arrest suspected persons. In the exercise of this power, the committee sent into Lincoln and Rowan counties, and had a number of persons arrested and brought before them. Those who manifested penitence for their toryism, and took an oath to support the cause of liberty and of the country, were discharged. Others were sent under guard into South Carolina for safe keeping. The meeting of the delegates at Charlotte and the proceedings which grew out of that meeting, produced the zeal and unanimity for which the people of Mecklenburg were distinguished during the whole of the Revolutionary War. They became united as a band of brothers, whose confidence in each other, and the cause which they had sworn to support, was never shaken, in the worst of times."

The above extract is copied from the eleventh chapter of the second volume of Martin's History of North Carolina.

In order to fully appreciate the discussion that is to follow it is important to bear in mind, as the historian says: First, that the delegates, assembled at

Charlotte, declared the county of Mecklenburg, North Carolina, independent of the crown of Great Britain; Second, they established a code of laws for managing their new government, and Third, placed a "Committee of Safety" in charge of the administration. All three of these things, remember, were done by one and the same convention on May 19-20, 1775.* The reason for thus emphasizing this fact will appear as we proceed.

Martin's History further declares that the proceedings at Charlotte were transmitted to Philadelphia for ratification by the Continental Congress, and that the President, deeming the subject of the resolutions "premature," declined to submit them to that body for consideration.

This unwillingness to recognize the Mecklenburg Declaration of Independence, we infer from the proceedings, was due to the fact that when the messenger, bearing the declaration, arrived in Philadelphia he found the Continental Congress not only opposed to independence individually, but actually preparing a petition to King George the Third, which was subsequently subscribed by every member on July 8, 1775, declaring, "We have not raised armies with the ambitious design of separating from Great Britain and establishing independent States." And, of course, any measure demanding secession from

---

*The delegates met on May 19, and John McKnitt Alexander, the secretary, says, "After sitting in the court-house all night, neither sleepy, hungry, nor fatigued," adopted the declaration "about 2 o'clock A. M., May 20." See Legislative Pamphlet in Appendix for Alexander's testimony.

the mother country received no consideration from Congress. Yet, notwithstanding the Continental Assembly, through its President, declined to sanction this bold action of the men of Mecklenburg, their new government was maintained just the same through its Committee of Safety, and British authority forever ceased at Charlotte, North Carolina, on May 20, 1775.

At the meeting of the delegates in Charlotte, John McKnitt Alexander was chosen secretary, and thus became custodian of the records. In April, 1800, twenty-five years after this meeting, these records, including the Mecklenburg Declaration, were burned with Alexander's dwelling. In the mean time, however, the old secretary, as he is called, had transcribed not less than five copies of the original resolutions, and, after the destruction of the declaration, Alexander made two additional copies from memory, and presented one of them to his friend, General William R. Davie. This memory transcript is known to historians as the "Davie copy." It contains many verbal errors, and, besides being written in the past tense, instead of the present, omits the sixth resolution. Alexander, however, confesses to a possible lapse of memory, when writing the Davie copy, in the following certificate upon its back:

"The foregoing statement, though fundamentally correct, may not literally correspond with the original record of the transactions of said delegation."*

---

*See Davie copy in archives of State University.

In 1819, two years after the death of John McKnitt Alexander, an account of the proceedings at Charlotte, including a duplicate of the Davie copy of the resolutions, was published in the *Raleigh Register*, by his son, Dr. Joseph McKnitt Alexander, with this note appended:

"The foregoing is a true copy of the papers, on the above subject, left in my hands by John McKnitt Alexander, deceased."

This publication was copied into the *Essex Register*, of Massachusetts, and referred by John Adams to Thomas Jefferson, whom it appears to have vexed greatly, as he wrote Mr. Adams: "And you seem to think it [the declaration] genuine. I believe it spurious. I deem it to be a very unjustifiable quiz."* In the same letter Mr. Jefferson also harshly criticises the patriotism of two of his associate members of Congress from North Carolina, accusing Hooper of toryism and Hewes of "wavering" in the American cause; forgetting that he himself, with every other member of Congress, was opposed to independence at the time the Mecklenburg Declaration was received in Philadelphia, as is evidenced by the petition, above quoted, which as already stated was subscribed by every delegate in that body on July 8, 1775.

With this letter of Mr. Jefferson, dated July 9, 1819, repudiating the Mecklenburg Declaration, began the controversy as to the genuineness of the resolutions. The friends of that venerable states-

---

*Page 314, vol. 4, Jefferson's works. This letter is also copied in the Legislative pamphlet. See Appendix.

man contending that it was impossible for John McKnitt Alexander to re-write the resolutions from memory, and that in his effort to do so he had confused the Mecklenburg and National declarations and introduced several phrases peculiar to the latter document. These friends were not aware, as will appear presently, that several genuine copies of the Mecklenburg resolutions were extant, and in the possession of historians and others long anterior to the burning of the records with Alexander's dwelling, and had Alexander refrained from making an autograph copy of the resolutions from memory, the declaration would still have been preserved and the long controversy caused by the Davie copy avoided.

And, although the followers of Mr. Jefferson allege that the Mecklenburg Declaration was never known previous to its publication in the *Raleigh Register* in 1819, there is abundant evidence to prove that at least seven authentic copies of those resolutions were in existence before the proceedings of the convention were burned in 1800. Of these seven transcripts, four, at the direction of the delegates, were transmitted to Congress at Philadelphia by John McKnitt Alexander, shortly after the meeting at Charlotte adjourned. One to the President, and one copy each to the three members from North Carolina. A fifth copy appeared in the *Cape Fear Mercury* in June, 1775, within thirty days after the declaration was adopted. A sixth copy was presented by Alexander to Dr. Hugh Williamson, who was then writing a history of the State, and Governor Stokes, in the preface to a pamphlet issued by the

DECLARATION OF INDEPENDENCE 19

Legislature of 1830-31, testifies to having seen that copy, with a letter from John McKnitt Alexander, in the possession of Williamson as early as 1793. And a seventh copy of the declaration, which the author says was obtained before 1800, the year the records were burned, is preserved in Martin's History of North Carolina.

It is with this seventh or Martin copy of the Mecklenburg Declaration that we propose to deal to-day. And it is well, therefore, before proceeding farther, to inquire who Martin was and ascertain his possible sources of information as to the convention at Charlotte on May 19-20, 1775.

According to his preface and the *North Carolina University Magazine* for April, 1893, Francois Xavia Martin in 1782, at the age of 20, came from France to New Berne, North Carolina, where he first taught school, then published a newspaper, and subsequently practised law. In 1791-92, by a resolution of the General Assembly, he was engaged to compile and publish the British Statutes, then in use in North Carolina, and in 1803 to edit and print the private acts of the Legislature. The character of this work and the collection of materials for a State history, which, the preface says, began to engage the attention of that author as early as 1791, required the presence of Mr. Martin at the State capitol, where he had access to the public documents and colonial records. There he saw much of William Polk, George Graham, and Joseph Graham, who witnessed the adoption of the Mecklenburg Declaration, and became personally acquainted with James

Harris and Robert Irwin, two of the delegates that signed the resolutions, as all five of these men, Wheeler's History says, were successively members of the Legislature from Mecklenburg County from 1791 to 1803, the time Mr. Martin was serving the State and collecting material for his book.

In 1806 Mr. Martin was chosen a member of the General Assembly for the borough of New Berne, when he was again associated with George Graham, who had been re-elected, and also with Nathaniel Alexander, who, at that time, was Chief Executive of North Carolina. Governor Alexander, besides being a citizen of Mecklenburg County, was a brother-in-law of Ephraim Brevard, who drew the declaration, and a son-in-law of Col. Thomas Polk, who read the resolutions aloud from the court-house steps, immediately after their adoption, to the large concourse of people that had assembled to witness the proceedings of the delegates.

Next, Mr. Martin's home was in Craven County, where he personally knew Richard Caswell, who lived in the adjoining county of Dobbs, as both men were lawyers and contemporary attorneys at the bar of New Berne, and the neighboring towns for several years, prior to the death of Caswell in 1789.

Richard Caswell is the man that represented the New Berne district in the Continental Congress from 1774 to 1776, and was a member of that assembly when Captain Jack, the bearer of the Mecklenburg Declaration to Congress, arrived in Philadelphia, and is known to have received a special copy of the resolutions from Jack. For, as before stated, that messenger had been directed by the delegates at Charlotte to deliver copies of the proceedings to the three members from North Carolina as well as the President of Congress. And, in acknowledging the receipt of a copy of the declaration, Caswell, in a joint letter with his colleagues Hewes and Hooper, predicted that the whole continent would soon follow Mecklenburg's example in declaring independence.

Further, Mr. Martin having been appointed a Federal judge, removed to Mississippi in 1809, and a year later was transferred to Louisiana. And, as we learn from his preface, had completed the manuscript of the first two volumes of his history, begun in 1791, prior to leaving North Carolina for the far South. These volumes, which recount the State's history, including the circumstances of the Mecklenburg Declaration, down to the summer of 1776, were taken by the author in manuscript to New Orleans, to await the completion of a third and a fourth volume, for which, the preface informs us, there were "very ample notes and materials." But owing to a busy life and feeble health after his arrival in Louisiana, and finding no opportunity for finishing volumes three and four of his book, Judge Martin, continues the preface, printed the manuscript of one and two without revision in 1829. Thus it is seen that, although Martin's History was not published until twenty years after it was written and ten years after Mr. Jefferson first questioned the authenticity of the Mecklenburg Declaration, the manuscript had been prepared 1791 to 1809 and shipped to New Orleans ten years before the beginning of the controversy. And this long delay in printing the manuscript—years after the appearance of the Davie copy—no doubt caused Mr. Bancroft and other noted historians, who evidently failed to read his preface, to undervalue Martin's account of what was done at Charlotte on May 19-20, 1775. Again, the adoption of the Mecklenburg Declaration is recorded in the last chapter of the last volume of Martin's History, and for that reason the "doubters" contend that this final chapter was added by the author after his book had been finished, in order to settle the controversy caused by the appearance of the Davie copy, which John McKnitt Alexander is known to have made from memory. If this contention of the opposition is true, the resolutions in Martin's History should be a copy of the Davie resolutions, with which they do not agree, for, according to Mr. Jefferson's friends, there was no Mecklenburg Declaration extant prior to 1819, when the Davie paper appeared in the *Raleigh Register*.

Next, Prof. Charles Phillips, one of Mr. Jefferson's most ardent supporters in the *North Carolina University Magazine* for May, 1853, not only declares that "the Martin copy of the declaration is evidently a polished edition of the Davie copy," but insinuates that the sixth resolution, which forms part of the Martin series, but not that of Davie, was added by the judge. Showing that Dr. Phillips, like many other students of this question, failed to examine Martin's preface, from which he would have discovered that the Martin resolutions are not only older than the Davie transcript, but that the

Declaration of Independence

Judge, finishing his book in 1809, ten years before the declaration controversy arose, had no incentive either to polish or amend the Mecklenburg resolutions. Besides, Judge Martin's reputation as a jurist and historian would have forbidden such trifling with history.

Further, the assertion that the chapter containing the declaration is a supplement to Martin's History is also contradicted by the arrangement of the book, which is written in annals—each event recorded under the year in which it happened. For example, chapter ten of the second volume is filled with events occurring in 1774-75 and chapter eleven, which describes the adoption of the Mecklenburg Declaration, with those of 1775-76. And the proceedings of the delegates at Charlotte are recorded under the year 1775, and followed by other incidents of North Carolina history in their chronological order, down to August, 1776, where the volume ends.

Again, Martin's manuscript is shown to have been neither revised nor enlarged after 1809, when the author became a citizen of Louisiana, by the fact that he refers to Captain Jack, in the extract from his history quoted in the opening of our address, as still living, where he says, "James Jack, then of Charlotte, but *now* residing in the State of Georgia, was engaged to be the bearer of the resolutions to the President of Congress." Yet we find in Hunter's Sketches of Western North Carolina that Jack died in 1822, seven years before Martin's History went to press. That the publication of Martin's book was deferred long after the author had written it and removed to the far South is made evident by the following assertion in the preface: "The determination has been taken to put the work to press in the condition it was when it reached New Orleans; this has prevented any use being made of Williamson's History of North Carolina (printed in 1812), a copy of which did not reach the writer's hands till after his arrival in Louisiana."

And the truthfulness of Martin's History is shown by the care with which the work was prepared. For example, at the close of each chapter the author cites the source or sources from which its contents were derived. And at the end of that describing the adoption of the Mecklenburg Declaration the reader is referred to "records, magazines, gazettes" as the contemporary publications from which the author's facts were obtained. And, of course, the newspaper from which the historian procured his account of the proceedings at Charlotte could have been no other than the *Cape Fear Mercury* of June, 1775, as that is the only gazette known to have printed the Mecklenburg Declaration of Independence prior to the writing of Martin's History or the burning of the original resolutions with John McKnitt Alexander's residence in April, 1800.

Additional proof that the copy of the resolutions, printed by Martin, were transcribed before the original series were burned with Alexander's residence, is furnished by the Rev. Francis L. Hawks, D. D., LL. D., whose reputation as a divine is a sufficient guarantee of his loyalty to the truth. On May 20, 1857, Dr. Hawks delivered the anniversary address of the twentieth of May celebration at Charlotte, and in the course of his remarks said that some years before, when he and Judge Martin resided in New Orleans, he asked that historian where and when he procured the copy of the Mecklenburg Declaration printed in his book, to which the Judge replied, "In the western part of the State, prior to the year 1800." Whether it was a manuscript or newspaper copy is not stated, but probably the latter, as Mr. Martin also said, "It was not obtained from Alexander."

Such is the history of Martin the historian. From it we have ascertained:

(1) That Martin was engaged from 1791 to 1809, nearly twenty years, in work which gave him official access to the public documents and colonial records of North Carolina, and, as his book states, he gleaned from the contemporary records, magazines, and gazettes all data pertinent to the Mecklenburg Declaration;

(2) That Martin possessed a copy of that declaration made before April, 1800, when the original resolutions were burned with John McKnitt Alexander's house, and had also read the proceedings of the delegates printed in the *Cape Fear Mercury* of June, 1775;

(3) That while collecting materials for his history Martin was daily associated with five members of the Legislature from Mecklenburg County that were present when the declaration was adopted—two of whom signed the resolutions. And Martin had previously known personally at least one mem-

ber of the Continental Congress that received a special copy of the declaration from the delegates at Charlotte; And

(4) That at the time Martin's account of the convention was prepared, 1791 to 1809, all the facts he recorded were to be had from living witnesses, a privilege seldom enjoyed by historians.

Having ascertained the possible sources of Martin's information, and seen the importance of examining the preface to a history before discrediting the author's narrative, we will now examine the data of Major Alexander Garden, who wrote "Anecdotes of the American Revolution," in which he corroborates Martin as to the date and action of the Mecklenburg convention, and learn Garden's opportunities for obtaining information upon that subject.

Alexander Garden was a citizen of Charleston, South Carolina, and an officer in Lee's famous legion, in which command page 235 of Wheeler's History of North Carolina says there were also troops from Mecklenburg County. Later Major Garden was appointed aide-de-camp to General Greene, where he was constantly associated with Thomas Polk, another member of Greene's staff. This being the same Colonel Polk who, immediately after signing the Mecklenburg Declaration, read the resolutions aloud to the large concourse of people that assembled at Charlotte on May 19-20, 1775, to witness the proceedings of the delegates. And at the close of the Revolutionary War Major Garden returned to his home in Charleston, to which city his

Mecklenburg comrade-in-arms made frequent journeys, as in those days Charleston was the market in which the farmers of that county sold their crops and the Charlotte merchants purchased goods. Freight was transported entirely with wagons, which required the presence of their owners in town to superintend the handling of their produce and merchandise. These constant visits of Mecklenburg veterans no doubt afforded Major Garden ample opportunity for ascertaining the facts as to the action of the delegates at Charlotte in May, 1775. Further, I am informed that Garden was a member of the Charleston Library, an important circumstance as we shall see farther on, and when collecting material for his anecdotes, thoroughly examined all the newspaper files of that institution, as is abundantly proved by the large number of extracts copied from them into his book. Besides, there were other avenues of information open to Major Garden, as in the same command with him during the Revolutionary War was his personal friend Dr. William Read, another citizen of Charleston. Dr. Read at one period of the war was a member of General Washington's staff, and in 1781 was appointed by Congress hospital physician for the Department of the South, with headquarters at Charlotte, North Carolina,* where he was for some time closely associated with Ephraim Brevard, who drew the Mecklenburg Declaration, and John McKnitt Alexander, the

---

*Doctor Toner's manuscript collection of "Biographical Data Regarding American Physicians," preserved in Congressional Library, Washington, D. C.

secretary of the convention that adopted it, as Brevard was a patient of Dr. Read in the home of Alexander for many weeks immediately preceding his death in 1781. And on page 181 of the appendix to his manuscript work upon the Mecklenburg Declaration of Independence, preserved in the Thwait Library at Madison, Wisconsin, Lyman Draper states that "Dr. Brevard," who had been a prisoner at Charleston, "when at length set at liberty, reached the home of his friend John McKnitt Alexander, where he lingered several months, his disease baffling the best medical skill, Dr. William Read, Physician General of the Southern Army, visiting him from Charlotte." And we are informed by Major Garden himself that some of the historical items in "Anecdotes of the American Revolution" were obtained from Dr. Read. For example, after describing the action of the delegates in May, 1775, Garden adds: "Of the zeal of the inhabitants in the vicinity of Charlotte and Salisbury in favor of the cause of their country, my friend Dr. William Read has recently given striking proof."

The first series of "Anecdotes of the American Revolution" were published by Garden in 1822, the second series in 1828, and the whole reprinted in three volumes in 1865. The circumstances of the Mecklenburg Declaration are narrated on pages 7, 8 and 9 of the third volume, and the account of the meeting at Charlotte is the same as that recorded by Martin, only more condensed, and like Martin's version evidently taken from the *Cape Fear Mercury* of June, 1775. For, upon comparing the two descriptions of the convention, as recorded in Martin's History of North Carolina and "Anecdotes of the American Revolution," the reader will find the date of the meeting, the language of the resolutions, and often whole sentences in the two narratives to be literally the same, thereby proving them to have come from a common source. And in neither account is there any evidence that Martin or Garden knew of the Davie copy of the Mecklenburg Declaration at the time their histories were written.

Garden could not have copied his narrative from Martin's History, for "Anecdotes of the American Revolution" was printed first, in 1828, and Martin's work one year later, 1829. Besides, in his address at Charlotte, before referred to, Dr. Hawks states that Judge Martin had told him that he did not give Garden a copy of the resolutions, or know that he possessed one. Neither could Martin have borrowed from Garden, for Martin announces in his preface that he "put the work to press in the condition it was when it reached New Orleans," in 1809, nearly twenty years before Garden's book was printed. Thus Martin and Garden, working independently of each other, and upon materials only in part the same, arrive at the same conclusion as to what was done at Charlotte on May 19-20, 1775. And in this connection it is well to remember that Martin and Garden, of all writers on this subject, are the only historians that personally knew men that were present when the declaration was made, and that Martin's History and "Anecdotes of the American

Revolution" are only discredited by doubting critics who have no personal knowledge of the events which Martin and Garden describe. Excepting the official papers of the Colonial Governor of North Carolina, which will be considered in their proper place, the earliest documentary reference to the Mecklenburg Declaration of Independence, of which there is any record, is found in "The Mecklenburg Censor," a poem written in 1777 by Adam Brevard, a brother of the author of the twentieth of May resolutions. The genuineness of the "Censor" is vouched for by Wheeler's History of North Carolina, Lyman Draper's manuscript in the Thwait Library, and Hon. David L. Swain, then president of the University of North Carolina, in whose possession the original poem was at the time of his death in 1868. And in the appendix of Draper's manuscript there is a copy of a letter from Governor Swain to Hon. George Bancroft, the historian, dated March 18, 1858, which reads: "The poem to which I refer above bears date March 18, 1777, extends through two hundred and sixty lines, and is of unquestionable authenticity. It opens as follows:

"THE MECKLENBURG CENSOR.

"When Mecklenburg's fantastic rabble,
Renowned for censure, scold and gabble,
In Charlotte met in giddy council,
To lay the constitution's ground-sill,
By choosing men both learned and wise,
Who clearly could with half shut eyes,
See mill-stones through or spy a plot,
Whether existed such or not;

DECLARATION OF INDEPENDENCE   31

>Who always could at noon define
>Whether the sun or moon did shine,
>And by philosophy tell whether,
>It was dark or sunny weather;
>And sometimes, when their wits were nice,
>Could well distinguish men from mice.
>First to withdraw from British trust,
>In congress, they, the very first,
>Their Independence did declare."

Here Adam Brevard, who witnessed the proceedings of the delegates, testifies over his own signature, less than two years after the meeting, that those delegates did "withdraw from British trust" earlier than the Continental Congress at Philadelphia.

The next proof, in chronological order, that Mecklenburg County declared her independence of Great Britain in May, 1775, is found in numerous deeds which were executed during and immediately after the Revolutionary War, and are now on file in the court-house at Charlotte. For after independence had been resolved upon by the men of Mecklenburg, and long before liberty was won by America, owing to the unsettled state of affairs, there was among the people of the county a great diversity as to the manner of drawing deeds. And, as no fixed standard of preparation was in vogue, as many as three different styles of these documents are preserved among the county records. Some of these transfers of property are dated "in the reign of King George the Third;" some, prepared by patriots of strong local pride, reckon the time of "our independence" from the Mecklenburg Declaration, while others recite the date of their execution from "American

Independence." "King George deeds" were not recorded after the year 1777, while those relating to "our independence" and "American Independence" were both registered as late as 1799, when, most of the county's Revolutionary veterans having passed away, the National Declaration became the sole standard.

These Mecklenburg Declaration indentures, of which we quote several, read:

(1) "This indenture made this 13th day of February, 1779, and in the fourth year of our independence." Page 15, book 36. Robert Harris, Register.

(2) "This indenture made this 28th day of January, in the fifth year of our independence and the year of our Lord Christ 1780." Page 29, book 1. William Alexander, Register.

(3) "This indenture made on the 19th day of May, and in the year of our Lord 1783, and the eighth year of our independence." Page 119, book 2. John McKnitt Alexander, Register.

(4) Peter Reap, forgetting that the Mecklenburg Declaration was only a county affair, dates the independence of his State from it as follows: "This indenture made the year of our Lord 1789, and on the 18th day of April, and being the 14th year of the independence of the State of North Carolina." Page 95, book 11. John McKnitt Alexander, Register.

As these deeds were executed and filed thirty and forty years prior to the Mecklenburg controversy, their testimony is incontrovertible. And be it remembered, that "our independence," repeated in those deeds, are the identical words, according to Martin's History, shouted by the vast throng of people that assembled in Charlotte on May 19-20, 1775, and demanded freedom of their delegates.*

Notwithstanding the claim of Mr. Jefferson's friends that the Mecklenburg Declaration was never heard of previous to the publication of the Davie copy in the *Raleigh Register* in 1819, we find its glories proclaimed by a school boy ten years anterior to that date, when James Wallis, a pupil of Sugar Creek Academy, three miles east of Charlotte, makes the following announcement in his declamation at the closing exercises of that institution on June 1, 1809. Wallis's recitation was printed in the *Raleigh Minerva* of August 10, 1809, and copied in part into the *Catawba Journal* of July 11, 1826, which latter paper is now in our possession, and credits the boy's address to the *Minerva* of the above date. Wallis in part said: "On May 19, 1775, a day sacredly exulting to every Mecklenburg bosom, two delegates, duly authorized from each militia company in the county, met in Charlotte. After a cool and deliberate investigation of the causes and extent of our differences with Great Britain, and taking a review of probable results, pledging their all in support of their rights and liberties, they solemnly entered into and published a full and determined Declaration of Independence, renouncing forever all allegiance, dependences or connection with Great

---

*See extract from Martin's History quoted at the opening of this discourse.

Britain—dissolved all judicial and military establishments emanating from the British crown and established others on principles corresponding with their declaration which went into immediate operation, all of which was transmitted to Congress by express and probably expedited the general Declaration of Independence. May we ever act worthy of such predecessors." This boy, James Wallis, bear in mind, gives substantially the same account of the Charlotte convention as Martin's History. That is, the delegates met in Charlotte on May 19, 1775, declared the county of Mecklenburg independent of Great Britain, established a code of laws for the new government, and sent the proceedings to the Continental Congress. Where did James Wallis get his facts? In 1809 neither Martin's History nor "Anecdotes of the American Revolution" had been printed, and the Davie copy was not published until 1819, ten years subsequent to that date. His only resource then was spectators and delegates to the convention, several of whom were then still living in the county, as John McKnitt Alexander, we know, survived until 1817, and John Davidson, another signer, until 1830, and a few of the spectators, who were much younger men, still longer.

In addition to this, the Rev. Samuel C. Caldwell, the head of Sugar Creek Academy and pastor of Sugar Creek Presbyterian Church, under whose auspices the school was conducted, married a daughter of John McKnitt Alexander in 1793, seven years anterior to the burning of the Mecklenburg Declaration with Alexander's residence, and no doubt Mr. Caldwell often saw the resolutions in the possession of his father-in-law, as tradition says they were a favorite topic of conversation with the "old secretary." The Rev. Caldwell was pastor of Sugar Creek Church from 1792 to 1826, and at the time of James Wallis's declamation, in 1809, had been in charge of that congregation about seventeen years. This gave that minister ample opportunity to become familiar with the circumstances of the Mecklenburg Declaration, as many of his flock had been present when it was adopted, and Abraham Alexander, the chairman of the delegates, was an elder in Sugar Creek Church for years previous to his death in 1786. And if Wallis's recitation had contained any errors, as to the proceedings of the delegates at Charlotte on May 19-20, 1775, Mr. Caldwell, in the fullness of his knowledge, would have corrected them before the address was repeated in public, as it was customary for the pupils to rehearse their "pieces" to the teacher preparatory to declaiming them at commencement.

Again, the date of the adoption of the Mecklenburg Declaration is determined by the following circumstance: On May 20, 1787, the twelfth anniversary of the meeting at Charlotte, there was born to Major John Davidson, one of the signers, a son, Benjamin Wilson. And in honor of the Mecklenburg Declaration Benjamin was called by his father "My Independence Boy," and to distinguish his identity in a county abounding in "Davidsons," was known among the neighbors as "Independence Ben." For this fact we are indebted to Mr. Robert F., aged seventy-five, and Dr. Joseph, aged sixty-eight years, sons of Benjamin Wilson Davidson, who now reside in Charlotte and are men of the highest integrity. Ben Davidson died when about forty-five years of age and is buried in Hopewell Cemetery, where his tombstone now stands with the date of his birth, May 20, 1787, inscribed upon it. In those days it was not unusual in Mecklenburg County to call children for public events, and we find Col. Thomas Polk, another signer, with a nephew named Thomas Independence, because born July 4, 1786.

Up to this stage of our investigations the evidences of the genuineness of the Mecklenburg Declaration of Independence range themselves in the following chronological order:

(1) The poem, "Mecklenburg Censor," of March 18, 1777;

(2) Birth of Benjamin Wilson Davidson on May 20, 1787;

(3) The deeds, executed during and immediately after the Revolutionary War, dating our independence from the Mecklenburg Declaration;

(4) Martin's History of North Carolina, written 1791 to 1809, in which the author cites contemporary records, magazines and gazettes as the authority for his account of the adoption of the Mecklenburg Declaration of Independence;

(5) "Anecdotes of the American Revolution," whose editor, Major Garden, personally knew Col. Thomas Polk and other Mecklenburg soldiers;

(6) The school boy's declamation of June 1, 1809;

(7) And the Davie copy of the resolutions, which, instead of being a cause for controversy, should be considered one of the best corroborative evidences of the genuineness of the Mecklenburg Declaration.

As we said near the beginning of our discourse, when a duplicate of the Davie copy was first printed in the *Raleigh Register* in 1819, by Dr. Joseph McKnitt Alexander, son of "the old secretary," the friends of Thomas Jefferson alleged that John McKnitt Alexander, in transcribing the resolutions from memory, confused the Mecklenburg and National Declarations. They also contended that no meeting, at which independence was proclaimed, was ever held in Charlotte on any day. And the more zealous of those partizans charged Dr. Joseph McKnitt Alexander with "tergiversation" in publishing the Mecklenburg Declaration at all, as it was "only an attempt to convict Mr. Jefferson of plagiarism, and thus rob him of the authorship of the first American Declaration of Independence." At the same time the friends and neighbors of John McKnitt Alexander rallied to the old secretary's support, but instead of trying to show the authenticity of the Mecklenburg Declaration as printed in the *Cape Fear Mercury* of June, 1775, they thoughtlessly undertook to prove the Davie copy of the resolutions to be verbally accurate, notwithstanding Alexander's certificate on the back of that transcript claimed them to be only "fundamentally correct." Thus the controversy was joined with more or less acrimony. And in this condition it remained for nearly twenty years, or until 1838, when the following resolutions were introduced into the discussion:

THE THIRTY-FIRST RESOLVES

"CHARLOTTETOWN, *Mecklenburg County,*
"May 31st, 1775.

"This day the Committee of this county met and passed the following resolves:—

"*Whereas,* By an address presented to His Majesty by both Houses of Parliament in February last, the American Colonies are declared to be in a state of actual rebellion, we conceive that all laws and commissions confirmed by or derived from the authority of the King and Parliament are annulled and vacated, and the former civil constitution of these colonies for the present wholly suspended. To provide in some degree for the exigencies of this county in the present alarming period, we deem it proper and necessary to pass the following resolves, viz:—

"I. That all commissions, civil and military, heretofore granted by the crown to be exercised in these colonies, are null and void, and the constitution of each particular colony wholly suspended.

"II. That the Provincial Congress of each Province, under the direction of the Great Continental Congress, is invested with all legislative and executive powers within their respective provinces, and that no other legislative or executive power does or can exist at this time in any of these colonies.

"III. As all former laws are now suspended in this Province, and the Congress has not yet provided others, we judge it necessary for the better preservation of good order, to form certain rules and regulations for the Internal Government of this county, until laws shall be provided for us by the Congress.

"IV. That the inhabitants of this county do meet on a certain day appointed by the Committee, and having formed themselves into nine companies (to wit: eight for the county and one for the town), do choose a colonel and other military officers, who shall hold and exercise their several powers by virtue of the choice, and independent of the crown of Great Britain, and former constitution of this province.

"V. That for the better preservation of the peace and administration of justice, each of those companies do choose from their own body two discreet freeholders, who shall be empowered each by himself, and singly, to decide and determine all matters of controversy arising within said company, under the sum of twenty shillings, and jointly and together all controversies under the sum of forty shillings, yet so as their decisions may admit of appeal to the Convention of the Select Men of the County, and also that any one of these men shall have power to examine and commit to confinement persons accused of petit larceny.

"VI. That those two select men thus chosen do jointly and together choose from the body of their particular company two persons to act as constables, who may assist them in the execution of their office.

"VII. That upon the complaint of any persons to either of these select men, he do issue his warrant directed to the constable, commanding him to bring the aggressor before him to answer said complaint.

"VIII. That these select eighteen select men thus appointed do meet every third Thursday in January, April, July and October at the Court-House in Charlotte, to hear and determine all matters of controversy for sums exceeding 40s., also appeals; and in case of felony to commit the persons convicted thereof to close confinement until the Provincial Congress shall provide and establish laws and modes of proceeding in all such cases.

"IX. That these eighteen select men thus convened do choose a clerk, to record the transactions of said convention, and that said clerk, upon the application of any person or persons aggrieved, do issue his warrant to any of the constables of the company to which the offender belongs, directing said constable to summon and warn said offender to appear before said convention at their next sitting, to answer the aforesaid complaint.

"X. That any person making complaint, upon oath, to the clerk, or any member of the convention, that he has reason to suspect that any person or persons indebted to him in a sum above forty shillings intend clandestinely to withdraw from the county without paying the debt, the clerk or such member shall issue his warrant to the constable, commanding him to take said person or persons into safe custody until the next sitting of the convention.

"XI. That when a debtor for a sum above forty shillings shall abscond and leave the county, the warrant granted as aforesaid shall extend to any goods or chattels of said debtor as may be found, and such goods or chattels be seized and held in custody by the constable for the space of thirty days, in which time, if the debtor fail to return and discharge the debt, the constable shall return the warrant to one of the select men of the company where the goods are found, who shall issue orders to the constable to sell such a part of said goods as shall amount to the sum due.

"That when the debt exceeds forty shillings, the return shall be made to the convention, who shall issue orders for sale.

"XII. That all receivers and collectors of quit rents, public and county taxes, do pay the same into the hands of the chairman of this Committee, to be by them disbursed as the public exigencies may require, and that such receivers and collectors proceed no further in their office until they be approved of by, and have given to this Committee good and sufficient security for a faithful return of such moneys when collected.

"XIII. That the Committee be accountable to the county for the application of all moneys received from such public officers.

"XIV. That all these officers hold their commissions during the pleasure of their several constituents.

"XV. That this Committee will sustain all damages to all or any of their officers thus appointed, and thus acting, on account of their obedience and conformity to these rules.

"XVI. *That whatever person shall hereafter receive a commission from the crown, or attempt to exercise any such commission heretofore received, shall be deemed an enemy to his country;* and upon confirmation being made to the captain of the company in which he resides, the said company shall cause him to be apprehended and conveyed before two select men, who, upon proof of the fact, shall commit said offender to safe custody, until the next sitting of the Committee, who shall deal with him as prudence may direct.

"XVII. That any person refusing to yield obedience to the above rules shall be considered equally criminal, and liable to the same punishment, as the offenders above last mentioned.

"XVIII. That these Resolves be in full force and virtue until instructions from the Provincial Congress regulating the jurisprudence of the province shall provide otherwise, or the legislative body of Great Britain resign its unjust and arbitrary pretensions with respect to America.

"XIX. That the eight militia companies in this county provide themselves with proper arms and accoutrements, and hold themselves in readiness to execute the commands and directions of the General Congress of this province and this Committee.

"XX. That the Committee appoint Col. Thomas Polk and Dr. Joseph Kennedy to purchase 300

pounds of powder, 600 pounds of lead, 1000 flints, for the use of the militia of this county, and deposit the same in such place as the Committee may hereafter direct.
"Signed by order of the Committee,
"EPH. BREVARD,
"Clerk of the Committee."

These Resolves appeared first in the *South Carolina Gazette and County Journal* on June 13, 1775, and on page 48 of his manuscript work Lyman Draper says were copied from that paper, in an abbreviated form, into the *New York Journal* of June 29, 1775, and *Massachusetts Spy* of July 12, 1775, and credited by those papers to that of Charleston. Then these Resolves disappeared and were entirely forgotten for more than sixty years, or until Col. Peter Force, of Washington City, found them, and announced the fact through the *National Intelligencer* in December, 1838. Nine years later, in 1847, Dr. Joseph Johnson discovered this entire series of resolutions in the *South Carolina Gazette and County Journal* deposited in the Charleston Library. And about the same time Mr. Bancroft, the historian, found a copy preserved in the British State Paper Office in London.

Owing to their date they are known as the Thirty-first Resolves, but beyond the fact of their having been first printed in the Charleston newspaper of June 13, 1775, to which publication all copies of them can be traced, we shall see, as we proceed, that there is not one iota of evidence that these resolutions were ever considered, much less passed, at Charlotte on May 31, 1775, the date of their supposed adoption. On the contrary, we shall find that spectators and delegates to the twentieth of May convention testify, and the official utterances of the Governor of North Carolina at the time show, that resolutions, identical in purpose with the Thirty-first Resolves, were passed on the same day, and immediately after, the Declaration of Independence was made. This of course left nothing to be done by the delegates on May 31, 1775.

Yet, with this abundance of evidence available, some of the partizans of Mr. Jefferson not only allege that there was never a Declaration of Independence made at Charlotte, but insist upon the authenticity of the date of the Thirty-first Resolves. This in spite of the fact that in a controversy lasting more than three-quarters of a century those partizans have never been able to produce one particle of evidence, documentary or otherwise, that corroborates the date of the Thirty-first Resolves. Whether this contention is due to a lack of information on the part of those partizans or owing to a hope that by their persistence they could persuade historians to accept as genuine the Thirty-first Resolves, which do not declare independence, in place of the Mecklenburg Declaration that does, and thereby relieve Mr. Jefferson of the suspicion of plagiarism when drawing the National Declaration, we can only conjecture. But we do know, however, that had those would-be-protectors of the ex-President examined the proceedings of the Continental Congress of July

2, 1776, they would have discovered that Richard Henry Lee, and not Mr. Jefferson, is responsible for the introduction of all of the phrases into the National Declaration that are common to it and the Mecklenburg document, except "our lives, fortunes and sacred honor," and consequently their chief is not needing defenders from the charge of plagiarism.

The Thirty-first Resolves premise as their foundation that by declaring the American Colonies to be in a state of actual rebellion the British Parliament has annulled and vacated all provincial laws and commissions derived from the King, and has for the present "wholly suspended the constitution of each particular colony." And the people of Mecklenburg County, according to the preamble, in order "to provide for the exigencies" thus arising, decide to adopt the Thirty-first Resolves for rules of conduct, as number 18 of that series has it, "until instructions from the Provincial Congress, regulating the jurisprudence of the province, shall provide otherwise, or the legislative body of Great Britain resign its unjust and arbitrary pretensions with respect to America." In other words, the Thirty-first Resolves are intended to be only a temporary substitute for British statutes which have been wholly suspended; not by the men of Mecklenburg, mind you, but by an act of the English Parliament. Whereas, in the declaration it is the citizens of Mecklenburg County, and not Parliament, who "do hereby dissolve the political bonds which have connected us with the mother country." Yet a recent historian, that either neglected to read their preamble or failed to comprehend its meaning, boldly asserts "that the Resolves of May 31 proclaimed the independence of the United Colonies," as if one small county of a province could usurp the authority of the Continental Congress. To appreciate how misleading and absurd is this historian's statement, it is only necessary to give the preamble of the Thirty-first Resolves a cursory examination.

Having learned the purpose of the Thirty-first Resolves, let us inquire into their origin and ascertain why they were never adopted in the form and on the date in which they are printed in the *South Carolina Gazette and County Journal* of June 13, 1775.

When the people of Mecklenburg County realized that all British authority in America had been wholly suspended "by both Houses of Parliament in February, 1775," they held frequent meetings, as the preamble of the Thirty-first Resolves declares, "To provide in some degree for the exigencies of this county in the present alarming period." "At one of these meetings," says Martin's History, "it was agreed to elect a committee of two delegates from each militia company in the county, with ample powers to adopt such measures as to them should seem best for the colony. These company committees were to meet in 'general committee' at Charlotte on the nineteenth of May. The forms of their proceedings and the measures to be proposed," continues Martin, "had been previously agreed upon by the men at whose instance the committees were assembled, and Dr. Brevard had drawn up the resolutions some time before." Those resolutions could not have been a Declaration of Independence, for the company committees had not been elected with the expectation of Mecklenburg County's seceding from the mother country, but on the contrary only to provide rules and regulations in place of those wholly suspended by the British Parliament.

Everything being arranged, the delegates met in Charlotte on the day appointed to consider the so-called Thirty-first Resolves. The Rev. Hezekiah James Balch, Dr. Brevard and William Kennon, according to Martin, had already addressed the general committee on the causes which made the adoption of those Resolves desirable, when the proceedings of the delegates were suddenly interrupted by the news of the battle of Lexington in Massachusetts, which had just arrived. "And this intelligence," to quote Martin's History, "produced the most decisive effect, and the large concourse of people that had assembled to witness the proceedings of the general committee all cried out: 'Let us be independent! Let us declare our independence and defend it with our lives and fortunes!'" To this end a committee was immediately appointed, "and this committee," Martin continues, "was composed of the men who had planned the whole proceedings, and had already prepared the resolutions which it was intended should be submitted to the general committee. Dr. Brevard had drawn up the resolutions some time before and now reported them with amendments, etc. They were unanimously adopted and subscribed by the delegates." Thus, it will be seen, the news of the battle of Lexington caused the Thirty-first Resolves, which were "meant to be purely provisional, temporary and contingent in their force and virtue," to be amended into a Declaration of Independence.

That this is what was done at Charlotte on May 19-20, 1775, can be demonstrated by comparing the declaration with the Thirty-first Resolves, as follows: In the preamble of the Resolves the American Colonies are declared to be in a state of actual rebellion, by both Houses of Parliament. When amended into Resolve one of the declaration this reads, "Invasion of our rights as attempted by the Parliament of Great Britain." Again, in that preamble and in Resolves one and three of the Thirty-first, all American laws and commissions derived from the King are said to be wholly suspended by act of Parliament. As amended into Resolve two of the declaration these same laws, etc., are abrogated by the general committee as follows: "We, the citizens of Mecklenburg County, do hereby dissolve the political bonds which have connected us with the mother country," etc. Next, Resolves four and five, of the Thirty-first, provide for the election of officers "by the inhabitants of this county," and declare that the powers of those officers shall be exercised "independent of the crown of Great Britain." As amended into Resolves four and five of the declaration, the laws which were in force, prior to the arrival of the news from Lexington, remained in *statu quo,* and the county officers, instead of being elected by the voters, were transferred from the royal to the new government, and "entitled to exercise the same powers and authorities as heretofore," the sudden change of fealty allowing no time for the election of officers. This precedent was followed on May 20, 1861, when North Carolina seceded from the Union, without displacing even a magistrate or a country postmaster.

Additional proof that the Thirty-first Resolves and the Declaration of Independence were presented to the general committee successively for consideration on one and the same day is contained in the testimony of the following spectators and delegates to the convention. For instance, General Joseph Graham, who witnessed the proceedings, writes Dr. Joseph McKnitt Alexander, son of the old secretary, on October 4, 1830: "One among other reasons offered" (for calling the convention) "was that the King or Ministry had by proclamation or some edict, declared the Colonies out of the protection of the British Crown," which is substantially the same cause, for assembling the delegates, that is given in the preamble of the Resolves of the Thirty-first. Then John McKnitt Alexander, the secretary of the general committee, in describing the proceedings at Charlotte on May 19-20, 1775, says that in addition to declaring independence, the delegates "also added a number of by-laws to regulate their conduct as citizens." The identical purpose of the Thirty-first Resolves. Again, in the same description Alexander declares: "From this delegation" (which made the Declaration of Independence) "originated the court of inquiry for this county." Which court we find provided for in Resolves six to eleven of the Thirty-first. Another spectator, John Simeson, writes Col. William Polk on January 20, 1820: "The same committee" (which declared independence) "appointed three men to secure all the military stores for the county's use—Thomas Polk, John Phifer, and Joseph Kennedy." Which is the sum and substance of Resolve twenty of the Thirty-first except as to Phifer. The Rev. Humphrey Hunter, also present on that day, testifies that, "Those Resolves" (the declaration) "having been concurred in, by-laws and regulations for the government of a standing committee of Public Safety were enacted and acknowledged." Again, George Graham, William Hutchison, Jonas Clark, and Robert Robinson, four eye-witnesses to the proceedings, unite in certifying: "That, at the time of the Mecklenburg Declaration, a committee of safety for the county were elected, who were clothed with civil and military power," as is provided for in the Thirty-first Resolves. The testimony of all these witnesses is contained in the Legislative pamphlet printed in the Appendix.

Further proof that a Declaration of Independence was adopted and county laws passed at one and the same session of the general committee is found in a contemporary proclamation of the Royal Governor, who read the proceedings at Charlotte soon after the delegates adjourned. This proclamation, which is dated August 8, 1775, and printed in volume ten of the North Carolina Colonial Records, recites: "Whereas I have also seen a most infamous publication in the *Cape Fear Mercury,* importing to be

DECLARATION OF INDEPENDENCE 51

Resolves of a set of people styling themselves a committee for the county of Mecklenburg, [first] most traitorously declaring the entire dissolution of the laws, government and constitution of this country, and [then] setting up a system of rule and regulation repugnant to the laws and subversive to His Majesty's government."

Next, Judge Martin, who cites contemporary records, magazines, and gazettes as authority for his statements, affirms in his history of North Carolina that, after resolving upon independence, "The delegates at Charlotte being empowered to adopt such measures as in their opinion would best promote the common cause [also] established a variety of regulations for managing the concerns of the county." The identical purpose of the Resolves of the Thirty-first.

Then Major Garden, the only historian except Martin that personally knew members of the general committee, in his "Anecdotes of the American Revolution" makes no mention of a meeting of delegates at Charlotte on May 31. This omission would be very remarkable if, as claimed by the followers of Mr. Jefferson, it was the resolves of that date, and not the Mecklenburg Declaration, that were adopted in May, 1775. Especially when we remember that at the time Garden wrote his book he was a member of the Charleston Library, in which was preserved a copy of the *South Carolina Gazette and County Journal* containing the Thirty-first Resolves. Garden could not have failed to read those resolutions when searching the newspaper files of that institution for historical incidents. So here is a historian with the Thirty-first Resolves and members of the general committee both accessible when preparing his anecdotes, yet he refers to no assembly of delegates on the thirty-first of May. The inference is easy. Garden was informed that the Declaration of Independence and the so-called Resolves of the Thirty-first were parts of one and the same proceedings on the 19th and 20th.

Again, although the *South Carolina Gazette and County Journal* was a tory paper, the editor does not comment upon the character of the Thirty-first Resolves, but simply inserts them in his journal without remark. Showing he was unwilling to vouch for either their accuracy or the supposed date of adoption.

Further, it must be universally conceded that neither the date nor the context of a newspaper article can be accepted as history when, like the Thirty-first Resolves, it can not be corroborated by even one witness. For example, the *New York Herald* of May 17, 1865, contains the following dispatch, dated Chester, South Carolina, May 12, 1865, at midnight: "To-day a detachment of Kilpatrick's cavalry proceeded to Buncombe County, N. C., and arrested Governor Vance at the home of his father-in-law," whereas the members of the Governor's family and his friends then residing in Statesville, Iredell County, North Carolina, testify that Vance was captured in that town on his birthday, May 13, 1865, while at dinner with his wife and children. Shall the future historian of North Carolina credit this unverified telegram in the *Herald,* or the citizens of Statesville that saw the federal soldiers remove Vance from their midst?

Through what channel the Thirty-first Resolves reached the *South Carolina Gazette and County Journal* is not known. It is probable, however, that some one at Charlotte, when writing to Charleston on May 31, 1775, enclosed to that paper a copy of the resolutions which Martin's History says Dr. Brevard had drawn up some time before the meeting on the nineteenth of May, and, as the resolutions were without date, the printer inserted that of the letter which accompanied them.

All contemporary witnesses, without an exception, including delegates and spectators and the Colonial Governor, who read the proceedings of the convention in print, shortly after it adjourned, testify that a Declaration of Independence was adopted, and laws for the new government enacted by the general committee at one and the same meeting. This left nothing to be done on May 31, 1775, and no one says there was a session of the delegates on that day except doubting critics who cannot produce even one witness to prove their contention. Yet those doubters will insist that it was the Thirty-first Resolves, and not the Mecklenburg Declaration, that was printed in the *Cape Fear Mercury* in June, 1775. Fortunately for us, the Royal Governor of North Carolina, at that time, has left among his colonial papers several such minute descriptions of the transactions of the delegates as published in the *Mercury,* that there is no mistaking the resolutions to which he refers. His first mention of the proceedings at Charlotte is contained in his address to the Executive Council on June 25, 1775, which is printed on pages 38 and 39, Volume 10, of the Colonial Records of North Carolina. There the Governor, after enumerating several disloyal occurrences in the province, continues: "And the late most treasonable publication of a committee in the county of Mecklenburg, *explicitly* renouncing obedience to His Majesty's government and all lawful authority whatsoever, are such audacious and dangerous proceedings, and so directly tending to the dissolution of the constitution of this province, that I have thought it indispensably my duty to advise with you on the measures proper to be taken for the maintenance of His Majesty's government and the constitution of this country, thus flagrantly insulted and violated." These remarks evidently do not refer to the Resolves of the Thirty-first, for we have already seen that those resolutions instead of "explicitly renouncing obedience to His Majesty's government," positively declare, in number 18 of that series, that they are only intended to "be in full force and virtue until * * * the legislative body of Great Britain resign its unjust and arbitrary pretensions with respect to America." While the declaration fulfils the Governor's description of the publication in the *Cape Fear Mercury* as follows, in Resolve two, "We the citizens of Mecklenburg County do hereby dissolve the political bonds which have connected us with the mother country, and absolve ourselves from all allegiance to the British crown."

DECLARATION OF INDEPENDENCE 55

Again, on page 48 of the same volume of those records there is a letter of the Governor written to Earl Dartmouth five days after the executive address and dated June 30, 1775, in which he remarks, "The Resolves of the committee of Mecklenburg, which your Lordship will find in the enclosed newspaper, surpass all the horrid and treasonable publications that the inflammatory spirit of this country has yet produced." Here again there is no allusion to the Resolves of the Thirty-first, for they, in place of being treasonable, expressly set forth in their preamble that their intention is merely "To provide in some degree for the exigencies of this county in the present alarming period." But the declaration teems with treason in Resolve three, where it proclaims "That we do hereby declare ourselves a free and independent people."

In the same letter the Colonial Governor tells Earl Dartmouth, "A copy of these Resolves, I am informed, were sent off by express to the Congress at Philadelphia, as soon as they were passed in the committee." And as nothing is said of Philadelphia in the Thirty-first Resolves, this Provincial Executive must have obtained his information as to the destination of the proceedings at Charlotte from Resolve six of the declaration, which he read in the *Cape Fear Mercury*. It directs, "That a copy of these resolutions be transmitted by express to the President of the Continental Congress, assembled in Philadelphia, to be laid before that body."

Another and a positive proof that what the King's Governor saw in the *Cape Fear Mercury* in June,

1775, was the Mecklenburg Declaration of Independence, and not the Thirty-first Resolves, is held in the unmistakable words of his contemporary proclamation. That manifesto, quoted in another connection, is printed on pages 144 and 145 of the same volume ten of the records, and recites, "Whereas I have also seen a most infamous publication in the *Cape Fear Mercury,* importing to be Resolves of a set of people styling themselves a committee for the county of Mecklenburg, most traitorously declaring the entire dissolution of the laws, government, and constitution of this country." No advocate of the genuineness of the Thirty-first Resolves is willing to admit that they declare "the entire dissolution of the laws, government, and constitution of this country," as that would be acknowledging them to be a Declaration of Independence, something which the doubters insist was never made at Charlotte, and therefore those advocates must confess that the Governor's proclamation has no reference to the resolutions of May 31, but to the Mecklenburg Declaration, which declares in Resolve four, "that the crown of Great Britain cannot be considered hereafter as holding any rights, privileges, or immunities amongst us." To recapitulate:

The Thirty-first Resolves, drawn by Dr. Brevard prior to the arrival of the news of the battle of Lexington, were intended as a substitute for laws wholly suspended by an act of the British Parliament;

Those in the *Cape Fear Mercury* were prepared in consequence of the conflict at Lexington, refer to

Declaration of Independence 57

that battle in their context, and declare the laws abrogated by the citizens of Mecklenburg County;

The Thirty-first Resolves are limited as to time and power;

Those in the *Cape Fear Mercury* are treasonable and permanent in their action;

"The Thirty-first Resolves," declares the Rev. Dr. Welling, "are meant to be purely provisional, temporary, and contingent in their force and virtue";

Those in the *Cape Fear Mercury*, according to the Royal Governor, proclaim "the entire dissolution of the laws, government, and constitution of this country";

The Thirty-first Resolves "do not contemplate anything like a formal or definitive separation from Great Britain";

While those in the *Cape Fear Mercury* are a Declaration of Independence.

The Colonial Records contain other references of the Royal Governor of North Carolina to the action of "the committee for the county of Mecklenburg," but we deem those cited sufficient to indicate which series of resolutions appeared in the *Cape Fear Mercury*.

Now that we know the Mecklenburg Declaration of Independence was published in the *Cape Fear Mercury* as early as June, 1775, let us inquire what became of that journal and ascertain why it cannot be produced.

As stated in his letter, the Provincial Governor of North Carolina transmitted this copy of the *Mercury* to Earl Dartmouth on June 30, 1775, and his Lordship filed it in the British State Paper Office in London. There the paper remained until 1837, or until the Mecklenburg controversy was well under way, and then disappeared under the following circumstances:

In March, 1837, the Rev. Francis L. Hawks, D. D., LL. D., printed a review of "Tucker's Life of Jefferson" in the *New York Review* for that month. And in his criticism Dr. Hawks announced that the Mecklenburg Declaration was first published in the *Cape Fear Mercury* in June, 1775, which paper was still preserved in the Colonial Archives in England. And, among other things, the distinguished reviewer charged Mr. Jefferson with having plagiarised several of the Mecklenburg phrases when drawing the National Declaration. This accusation so greatly incensed the adherents of the venerable ex-President that Lyman Draper, in his manuscript, says the *Cape Fear Mercury* containing the proceedings at Charlotte was loaned to Hon. Andrew Stevenson, a friend of Mr. Jefferson, and never returned.

Mr. Stevenson, according to Appleton's Cyclopedia of American Biography, was a contemporary of Thomas Jefferson, and no doubt his personal friend. For he was born in Virginia in 1784, belonged to the same Democratic party, and was a prominent member of the State Legislature and of Congress for twenty years during the latter part of Mr. Jefferson's life, and in 1836 became Minister to England.

DECLARATION OF INDEPENDENCE

What Mr. Stevenson wanted with the *Cape Fear Mercury* or what he did with it, we do not know, as he neither published its contents, nor, so far as we can discover, informed any one that he had seen that paper. All of which seems very remarkable when we are told, in the same manuscript of Lyman Draper, that Jared Sparks, the historian, visited London in search of that copy of the *Mercury* in 1840-41, and of course must have made the acquaintance of Mr. Stevenson, who was at the time this government's representative at the Court of St. James.

In 1838, the year after Mr. Stevenson borrowed the *Cape Fear Mercury*, Col. Peter Force, remember, found the Thirty-first Resolves, which discovery intensified the controversy as to the genuineness of the Mecklenburg Declaration. This renewed discussion was continued in the press of the country, by citizens of Virginia and others, for some years, yet nowhere do we find that Mr. Stevenson ever participated in the debate, although, with the *Cape Fear Mercury* in his possession, he could have settled the controversy for all time. Mr. Stevenson, on his return to America, became rector of the University of Virginia, and died near there in 1857, having lived twenty years after finding the *Cape Fear Mercury*, without divulging its contents.

The loss of the *Cape Fear Mercury* from the British State Paper Office in London is accounted for on page 54 of Draper's manuscript as follows: "A note in pencil contained this memorandum, 'Taken out by Mr. Turner for Mr. Stevenson,

August 15, 1837.' It was evidently never returned. The person referred to, for whose use it had been taken, was Andrew Stevenson of Virginia, then Minister to the Court of St. James. Upon Colonel Wheeler's return to this country he applied to Hon. J. W. Stevenson of Kentucky, son of the deceased Minister to England, concerning the missing copy of the *Cape Fear Mercury,* and the answer was, though the missing copy could not be found, dispatches and other memoranda among the deceased Minister's papers indicates that the copy had once been in his possession."

That Mr. Stevenson was suspected of more than a passing interest in the Mecklenburg controversy, while Minister to the Court of St. James, is ascertained from the following paragraph in "Memorials of North Carolina," published in 1838, while Mr. Stevenson was still a resident of London. The author, J. Seawell Jones, who has evidently heard of the disappearance of the *Cape Fear Mercury* from the British Archives in August, 1837, gives way to his vexation thus: "It has been intimated to me by a friend that the present Envoy Extraordinary of the Government of the United States near the throne of England, had been entrusted with a commission to explore the archives of the Colonial Office, for evidence against the Mecklenburg Declaration. Under whose superintendence and advice, this exploring expedition was got up, it does not behoove me to say, but I can certainly wish its worthy commander whatever success he may deserve. He may depend upon his deserts being fairly and thoroughly canvassed whenever the fruits of his expedition shall be disclosed to the public." Thus the loss of the *Cape Fear Mercury* raises a presumption against the parties who obtained it and withheld it from their opponents and the public.

Among other arguments to disprove the authenticity of the Mecklenburg Declaration it is customary for the doubters to cite the time of Captain Jack's arrival in Salisbury as a "settler." And on page 227 of the *Magazine of American History* for March, 1889, the Rev. J. C. Welling, D. D., supposing Captain Jack, the bearer of the Mecklenburg Declaration to the Continental Congress for ratification, to have left Charlotte immediately upon the adjournment of the delegates, remarks: "An express rider carrying to Philadelphia a copy of important proceedings had at a meeting in Charlotte on May 20, and arriving in Salisbury, forty miles from Charlotte, early in the month of June, would move the 'inextinguishable laughter of the gods' in Homer." Whereas the manner in which this scholarly writer ignores adverse testimony is enough to fell those deities with nervous prostration. Had he but examined the statement of John McKnitt Alexander, the secretary of the convention, printed in the Legislative Pamphlet, a copy of which can be found in the Appendix, Dr. Welling would have ascertained that Jack, instead of leaving Charlotte on May 20, was not engaged as messenger until several days after that date. For Alexander, after describing the adoption of the declaration, says: "In a few days, a deputation of said delegation convened, when Capt. James Jack, of Charlotte, was deputed as express to the Congress at Philadelphia," etc. And in the same pamphlet Alexander is corroborated by George Graham, William Hutchison, Jonas Clark, and Robert Robinson, four citizens of Mecklenburg County, and all eye-witnesses to the proceedings of the delegates. As after relating the circumstances of the declaration, these men unite in testifying that, "We do further certify and declare that in a few days after the delegates adjourned, Capt. James Jack, of the town of Charlotte, was engaged to carry the Resolves to the President of the Congress, and to our representatives—one copy each; and that his expenses were paid by a voluntary subscription." Thus, upon the testimony of five contemporary witnesses, it appears that Jack was not selected as messenger to Congress until some days after the declaration was adopted, and was then detained, we do not know how much longer, until a voluntary subscription could be raised in the small village of Charlotte and the sparsely settled county of Mecklenburg, to defray his expenses of the journey. And that no doubt is why Jack declares in his affidavit, also printed in the Legislative pamphlet, he did not set out till "the following month."

Having traced the controversy from Mr. Jefferson's letter, dated July 9, 1819, repudiating the Mecklenburg Declaration, to the loss of the *Cape Fear Mercury* from the British Archives, on August 15, 1837, we will now turn our attention to the North Carolina Provincial Congress, upon the pro-

DECLARATION OF INDEPENDENCE 63

ceedings of which the doubters chiefly rely to discredit the Charlotte convention of May 19-20, 1775.

This Provincial Assembly met at Hillsborough on August 20, 1775, and among its delegates were four signers of the Mecklenburg Declaration. And the would-be defenders of Mr. Jefferson, from supposed plagiarism, contend that the proceedings of this Hillsborough Congress were so thoroughly loyal to King George the Third, that it was not only inconsistent, but utterly impossible, for men that had subscribed the twentieth of May resolutions to be members of this body. Both on account of the oath or "test" required for membership, and the character of the proceedings of the delegates. And, therefore, argue these would-be defenders, as those four men of Mecklenburg did serve as members of this Provincial association, there never could have been a Declaration of Independence made at Charlotte. These repudiators, forgetting that their argument applies with equal force to the so-called Thirty-first Resolves, which the doubters contend were the only resolutions ever adopted by Mecklenburg County, as those same Resolves direct, in rule four, that the affairs of the community shall be conducted "independent of the crown of Great Britain."

After observing how much in error were the positive assertions of the Jefferson partizans, as to which series of resolutions appeared in the *Cape Fear Mercury* in June, 1775, we are not willing to accept, without examination, their bold declarations as to the loyal sentiment pervading the test oath and proceedings of this Hillsborough Congress.

A review of the situation shows that in 1775 rebellion was so rife in North Carolina that within one week after Mecklenburg County declared itself independent of Great Britain, Abner Nash, at the head of a committee of his neighbors, frightened the King's Governor from New Berne, the seat of government, His Excellency taking refuge in Fort Johnston on the Cape Fear River, from whence he was driven, sixty days later, on board the British gunboat *Crusier,* by Col. John Ashe, who, with a large body of men, destroyed the fort and carried away the guns. "Fifty days after the adoption of the Mecklenburg Declaration," says the editor of the Colonial Records of North Carolina, "a public call was made for the election of delegates to this Hillsborough Provincial Congress," upon which the doubters so firmly rely to discredit the Mecklenburg Declaration. And as affairs of the last importance were to be submitted to it, a large representation of the people was said to be desirable. "In ninety days from that declaration," says the same editor, "in spite of a furious proclamation from the Royal Governor, issued from the man-of-war *Crusier,* forbidding the people to elect delegates to this same Hillsborough Congress, and offering a reward for the arrest and delivery of the leaders of the movement to the British authorities, elections were held throughout the entire province, delegates were duly chosen, and the congress met in open session at the time and place appointed. Everybody," continues the editor of the records, "understood the nature of the affairs to be submitted to the convention and appreciated their vital importance. And, as desired, an unprecedentedly large number of delegates were selected to consider them. Two hundred and fourteen delegates were elected in all, and one hundred and eighty-four of them were present. Every one of the thirty-five counties, into which the province was then divided, was represented, and every borough town. The congress was in session just twenty days and busy enough." Its proceedings are recorded on pages 164 to 220, inclusive, of Volume 10 of the Colonial Records of North Carolina.

In addition to the four signers of the Mecklenburg Declaration, there were among the delegates chosen, Cornelius Harnett, Robert Howe, Samuel Ashe, and Abner Nash, all of whom, according to page 98, Volume 10 of the Colonial Records, the King's Governor, in a letter dated July 16, 1775, one month previous to the assembling of this Provincial Congress, writes Earl Dartmouth advising the British authorities to "proscribe, as persons who have marked themselves out as proper subjects for such distinction in this colony, by their unremitting labors to promote sedition and rebellion here, from the beginning of the discontents in America, to this time, that they stand foremost among the patrons of revolt and anarchy." Who would expect to find loyalty to King George the Third in a Provincial Congress, composed of such delegates, elected under such circumstances? And to show how mistaken the doubters are in their estimate of that convention, we will now review its proceedings and ascertain whether its transactions were enacted for or against the interests of Great Britain.

The congress met on Sunday, August 20, 1775, and for lack of a quorum adjourned to the following day. Then Samuel Johnston, who had issued the call for what the Governor terms this "illegal assembly," was chosen moderator, and a resolution immediately adopted declaring that those of the Regulators who had fought the King's army at the battle of Alamance, four years before, and still remained unpardoned, "ought to be protected from every attempt to punish them by any means whatever, and that this congress will to their utmost protect them from any injury to their persons or property, which may be attempted on the pretense of punishing the said late insurrection or anything in consequence thereof." A sentiment, no doubt, universal among the signers of the Mecklenburg Declaration.

On the second day of the session a committee was appointed to inquire into the conduct of John Coulson, who had been "charged with dangerous practices against the liberties of America." But on no day do we find in the proceedings was any investigation made by this Provincial Congress as to the "dangerous practices" against the rights of Great Britain. On the third day the following oath, known as the "test" of loyalty to America, was adopted and subscribed by the delegates:

"We, the subscribers, professing our allegiance to the King, and acknowledging the constitutional executive power of government, do solemnly profess, testify and declare that we do absolutely believe that neither the Parliament of Great Britain, nor any member or constituent branch thereof, have a right to impose taxes upon these colonies to regulate the internal police thereof; and that all attempts, by fraud or force, to establish and exercise such claims and powers, are violations of the peace and security of the people, and ought to be resisted to the utmost.

"And that the people of this province, singly and collectively, are bound by the acts and resolutions of the Continental and Provincial Congresses, because in both they are freely represented by persons chosen by themselves; and we do solemnly and sincerely promise and engage, under the sanction of virtue, honor and the sacred love of liberty, and our country, to maintain and support all and every the acts, resolutions and regulations, of the said Continental and Provincial Congresses, to the utmost of our powers and abilities. In testimony whereof, we have hereto set our hands this 23d of August, 1775."

Such is the test or oath that the Jefferson followers claim destroys all possibility to there having been a Declaration of Independence at Charlotte, and go so far as to declare it infamous, if Mecklenburg had made the declaration in question, that her delegates should have subscribed this test.

In a number of monographs against the authenticity of the Mecklenburg Declaration the first paragraph only of this test is cited as evidence to that effect, while the writers shout, with their exclamation marks, "no signer of the Mecklenburg Declaration could subscribe to that!" Whereas, had those doubters been frank enough to print the entire test, their readers would have seen that no loyal son of Great Britain could take that oath. And, as the last paragraph of the test, like the codicil to a will, annulled all conflicting clauses, the delegates, as their proceedings prove, considered themselves bound only by that. Again, had the members of this North Carolina Provincial Congress deemed themselves loyal subjects of England, instead of requiring a test as a qualification for a seat in that assembly, only the usual oath, administered to all British subjects when inducted into office, would have been exacted of the delegates. But, on the contrary, this test was considered so essential, by this Hillsborough Congress, that it was required of all officials under that congress, without distinction of person in this and the succeeding body of April 4, 1776. Even after the passage of the famous resolutions, on April 12, 1776, instructing the delegates from North Carolina in the Continental Congress to vote for American independence, we read in the journal of April 15, 1776, that "William Hooper and John Penn, Esqs., delegates of the Continental Congress, and members of this House, appeared, *subscribed the test,* and took their seats." And it may be a matter of surprise to the scrupulous of this late day, that Messrs. Hooper and Penn, good Episcopalians, should thus unnecessarily involve their consciences by taking this test of loyalty to the King, if such it was, after they had been instructed to vote for independence, and then, within three months, giving their votes and subscriptions to the National Declaration. But thus it appears on record.

Saving the first two lines, probably thrown in for the sake of the scrupulous or disaffected members of the Provincial Congress, this test contains an emphatic denial of all authority of Parliament over the Colonies. And, declaring that authority should be resisted to the utmost, solemnly engages or agrees to maintain and support only all and every the acts, regulations, and resolutions of the Continental and Provincial Congresses.

The journal of this Hillsborough Congress has always been regarded by the people of North Carolina as a noble monument of the patriotism and wisdom of the men who were its members. It has been very largely extracted from by Judge Martin, in his history of the State, and he discovered nothing in the test irreconcilable with the Mecklenburg Declaration, which document he most emphatically affirms. And an incontrovertible proof that the test was regarded as an oath of disloyalty to Great Britain, by both British and American authorities, is recorded on pages 382 and 383, Volume II of Martin's History, where the author describes a truce conducted between a Continental and a British commander near Cross Creeks, now Fayetteville, North Carolina, in February, 1776. It reads: "General McDonald marched at first towards Colonel Moore, and halted, at some distance from his camp; he sent an officer, charged with a letter to the Colonel, bewailing the difficulty of his situation, and pressed, by his duty to the sovereign, to the fatal necessity of shedding blood, while led by the principles of humanity he wished the event might be prevented, by the submission of the Colonel and his party to the constitution and laws of their country; he enclosed a copy of the governor's proclamation and his own manifesto, expressing the hope, that the Colonel would coolly, impartially, and deliberately weigh their contents, and pay them that regard that they justly merited, from every friend of the human species; he proffered to him, his officers and men in the King's name, a free pardon and indemnity for all past transgressions, on their laying down their arms and taking the oath of allegiance, and concluded, that unless these terms were accepted, he must consider them as traitors to the constitution, and take the necessary steps to conquer and subdue them.

"Desirous of gaining time, Colonel Moore (who with his men had been enlisted by this North Carolina Provincial Congress) amused the General, till he could no longer temporize; he then replied that his followers and he were engaged in a noble cause, the most glorious and honorable in the world, the defense of the rights of mankind; they needed no pardon. In return for the Governor's proclamation, he enclosed a copy of the test required by the late Provincial Congress, to be subscribed by every officer in the province, invited him to subscribe and offer it for the signature of his officers, and on their doing so and laying down their arms, he promised to receive them as brothers; but concluded that in case of their refusal, the General and his men could only expect that treatment with which he had been pleased to threaten him and his followers."

At this stage of the proceedings American reinforcements arrived, and in a few days the General with the oath of allegiance was the prisoner of the Colonel with the test. Thus we have the test and the oath of allegiance contrasted in such a way that there is no mistaking their difference, even by a doubter of the Mecklenburg Declaration of Independence.

Having seen how the men that subscribed it, and the British Government understood the test, let us return to the proceedings of the Provincial Congress at Hillsborough that made it.

On the fourth day of the session, instead of inviting the King's Governor to return to the Capitol, and resume the executive duties, from which he had been chased by some of these very delegates, the congress created a committee to report a plan of Provincial Government rendered necessary, it was said, by "His Excellency the Governor refusing to exercise the functions of the office, by leaving the province and retiring on board a man-of-war, without any threats or violence to compel him to such a measure." As remarked by the editor of the Colonial Records, "The impudence of this is simply sublime."

On the fifth day the congress took into consideration the proclamation of the Governor, issued from the sloop-of-war *Crusier,* in the Cape Fear River, where His Excellency had taken refuge when driven from New Berne and Fort Johnston. In this manifesto the election of delegates to this Hillsborough assembly had been forbidden as follows: "I do hereby advise, forewarn and exhort all His Majesty's subjects within this province, to forbear making any choice of delegates to represent them in the intended convention at Hillsborough, as they would avoid the guilt of giving sanction to an illegal assembly acting upon principles subversive of the happy constitution of this country, and that they do by every means in their power oppose that dangerous and unconstitutional assembly and resist its baneful influence." And in order to show their contempt for this British Governor, the delegates directed his proclamation to "be burned by the common hangman."

On August 28, 1775, the ninth day of the session, the Committee of Intelligence reported the case of Dunn and Boote, two loyal attorneys residing in Salisbury that had undertaken to detain Captain Jack, the bearer of the Mecklenburg Declaration, when he passed through that town on his way to Philadelphia. When the news of the attempt of these lawyers upon Jack reached Charlotte, shortly thereafter, the Committee of Safety, at the head of Mecklenburg's new government, sent a posse to Salisbury and arrested Dunn and Boote. The prisoners were brought before the Committee of Safety at Charlotte, and upon trial and conviction, there being no suitable prison nearer, were taken to Charleston, South Carolina, and confined to jail. At the time of the seizure Dunn was attorney for the crown at Rowan County court. In the hope of procuring their release, the wives of Dunn and Boote had presented a petition to this North Carolina Provincial Congress. But the delegates, influenced, no doubt, by the Mecklenburg members, upon investigation, decided that imprisonment was "necessary and justifiable" and refused to liberate them.

On September 1st it was resolved that the colony be immediately put in a state of defense and that one thousand regular troops be raised to fight the King's army. On the second of the month William Hooper, Richard Caswell, and Joseph Hewes were chosen to represent North Carolina in the Continental Congress, which body, in the language of the Colonial Governor, was "another illegal assembly."

On September 4th the King's Governor, through his secretary, Mr. Biggleston, sought permission from this Provincial Congress to remove his household effects from New Berne to his place of refuge on board the *Crusier,* and send his coach and horses to the home of Farquard Campbell, a member of the congress. And the delegates resolved: "That if Mr. Biggleston should think proper to remove on board the man-of-war all of the Governor's effects, as well as his coach and horses * * * this congress is ever ready to give them * * * every safeguard and security; but as Mr. Farquard Campbell, a member of this congress, has expressed a sincere desire that the coach and horses should not be sent to his house in Cumberland, and is amazed that such a proposal should have been made without his approbation or privity, they conceive that they can by no means suffer the coach and horses to be removed to Cumberland County." And then further resolved: "That Farquard Campbell, Esq., hath, in the opinion of this congress, conducted himself as an honest member of society and a friend to the American cause; and that any confidential expressions that have been dropped by Governor Martin or any of his friends with respect to any reliance they may have upon the services of the said Farquard Campbell against the American cause, have been without any encouragement from the said Farquard Campbell, but have been made use of in order to bring his character into distrust and lessen the esteem, which, for his faithful services, he deserves from the inhabitants of this province." What queer resolutions and proceedings these would be if, as claimed by the Jefferson partizans, the delegates, in order to become members of this Provincial Congress, had taken an oath that was a test of loyalty to British authority?

On Friday, September 8, the delegates, after spending two weeks in declaring that they and their constituents would obey only the acts and regulations of the Provincial and Continental Congresses. would protect the survivors of the battle of Alamance from punishment by Great Britain, after trying John Coulson for "dangerous practices against the liberties of America," appointing a committee to report a plan of government subversive of British authority, burning His Excellency's proclamation by the common hangman, raising troops to fight the royal army and spending their time in adopting many other measures inimical to the King and Parliament, adopted an address to the inhabitants of the British Empire containing this remarkable paragraph: "We have been told that independence is our object; that we seek to shake off all connection with the parent State. Cruel suggestion! Do not all our professions, all our actions uniformly contradict this? We again declare and we invoke that Almighty Being who searches the recesses of the human heart and knows our most secret intentions, that it is our most earnest wish and prayer to be restored, with the other united Colonies, to the state in which we and they were placed before the year 1763."

This address, to the inhabitants of the British Empire, appears to have had about the same effect upon the Provincial Congress that a sermon does on the average congregation—all drop their sins, listen attentively to the preacher, approve of all he says, sing the long metre doxology with a gusto, and move out to resume their wickedness where they left off Saturday night. And, like many a sermon, the effect of this address was not felt beyond the walls within which it was uttered, and there is no evidence that it was ever transmitted to the people for whom it was made. It was probably prepared by some of those very delegates who, after chasing the Governor away, resolved in this Hillsborough convention that His Excellency the Governor had left the Province and retired on board a man-of-war *"without any threats or violence to compel him to such a measure."* Evidently there were wags in this congress.

On the next day, Saturday, September 9, after having been delivered of their "heartfelt effusions," and feeling better for the accouchment, the delegates, like the aforesaid congregation, returned to their sedition and rebellion, and organized a war establishment, as "a sincere earnest of our present and future intention" to fight the army of His Majesty King George the Third, notwithstanding "all our professions, all our actions uniformly contradict this." And, to insure success, not only "invoked that Almighty Being, who searches the recesses of the human heart and knows our secret intentions," but also appointed Thomas Polk, Adam Alexander, John Phifer, and John Davidson, four signers of the Mecklenburg Declaration of Independence, among other field officers.

In spite of this address to the inhabitants of the British Empire, the remainder of Saturday and the ensuing Sunday, the last two days of the session, as the journal shows, were spent by these same delegates in entirely severing North Carolina from the mother country and adopting a constitution for the administration of the executive, legislative, and the judicial affairs of the province, independent of the crown of Great Britain. And, as the editor of the Colonial Records in this connection remarks: "The die was now cast, and North Carolina at last a self-governing commonwealth, whose rights and liberties and privileges her people were ready to defend with their fortunes and lives, and all this by the most deliberate, well-considered action on the part of that same people, after a campaign of forty days, in which delegates, in numbers without a parallel then or since, were elected, nobody being taken by surprise, but everybody knowing that the assembly of men thus elected would bring matters to a crisis. And this was done full eight months before the Continental Congress advised the Colonies to change the form of their governments. It is worthy of note, too, that both New Hampshire and Massachusetts, following the example of North Carolina, justified the changes they made at subsequent periods by reason of the flight of their Governors. The more the action of this great Hillsborough Congress is studied, and the events immediately preceding, the more wonderful seems the deliberate, well-considered resolute boldness of our ancestors."

The signers of the Mecklenburg Declaration, in this Hillsborough convention, could have desired nothing better than was planned and executed by this Provincial Congress.

They might well have said to their people at home, "Our strength is to sit still." The Congress was effecting all they desired, and at its spring session the men of Mecklenburg had the great satisfaction to see this congress nobly resolve on American independence, as their county had done on May 19-20, 1775, before the representatives of any other colony had taken this decisive step. Congress met at Halifax on April 4, 1776, and, according to its journal, "On the 8th it was resolved, that Mr. Harnett, Mr.

Allen Jones, Mr. Burke, Mr. Nash, Mr. Kinchen, Mr. Person, and Mr. Thomas Jones be a select committee to take into consideration the usurpations and violences attempted and committed by the King and Parliament of Great Britain against America, and the further measures to be taken for frustrating the same, and for the better defense of this Province." On April 12, 1776, the select committee reported: "It appears to your committee that pursuant to the plan concerted by the British Ministry for the subjugation of America, the King and Parliament of Great Britain have usurped a power over the persons and properties of the people unlimited and uncontrolled; and disregarding their humble petition for peace, liberty and safety, have made divers legislative acts denouncing war, famine and every species of calamity against the continent in general. The British fleets and armies have been and still are daily employed in destroying the people, and committing the most horrid devastations on the country. The Governors in different colonies have declared protection to slaves who should imbrue their hands in the blood of their masters. That the ships belonging to America are declared prizes of war, and many of them have been violently seized and confiscated. In consequence of all which multitudes of the people have been destroyed, or from easy circumstances reduced to the most lamentable distress. And whereas, the moderation hitherto manifested by the united colonies, and their sincere desire to be reconciled to the mother country on constitutional principles, have procured no mitigation of the aforesaid wrongs and usurpations, and no hopes remain of obtaining redress by these means alone, which have been hitherto tried, your committee are of opinion the House should enter into the following resolve, to wit:

"*Resolved,* That the delegates from this colony in the Continental Congress be empowered to concur with the delegates of the other colonies in declaring Independency, and forming foreign alliances, reserving to the colony the sole and exclusive right of forming a constitution and laws for this colony, and of appointing delegates from time to time (under the direction of a general representation thereof) to meet the delegates of the other colonies for such purposes as shall be hereafter pointed out.

"The congress taking the same into consideration unanimously concurred therewith."

Thus we see, in practical results, the Hillsborough Provincial Congress was the proper association in which men who had signed the Mecklenburg Declaration of Independence should serve their country.

This completes our investigations as to the adoption and loss of the Mecklenburg Declaration of Independence, and the controversy regarding its genuineness. From a review of the evidence we have learned that on May 20, 1775, the citizens of Mecklenburg County, North Carolina, declared themselves independent of the crown of Great Britain. That the original copy of the resolutions was burned with John McKnitt Alexander's residence in the year 1800. In the same year Alexander made a transcript of that declaration from memory, which is known among historians as the Davie copy. In 1819, after the death of the old secretary, his son printed an account of the Mecklenburg convention in the *Raleigh Register*. This publication fell into the hands of Thomas Jefferson, who denied its authenticity, and caused a controversy between his friends and those of Alexander, the former contending that John McKnitt Alexander had confused the Mecklenburg and Philadelphia resolutions. Then Alexander's followers, instead of trying to show that there had been a Declaration of Independence at Charlotte, undertook to prove the verbal accuracy of the Davie copy, although Alexander himself had certified on its back that the Davie paper was only "fundamentally correct." And with the Jefferson champions alleging that the Mecklenburg Declaration was never heard of previous to the Raleigh publication in 1819, and the Alexander defenders insisting upon the accuracy of the memory copy, the controversy was kept up until 1838, when the Thirty-first Resolves were discovered. Then the doubters shouted, with great glee, that they had found what Alexander was trying to remember when he wrote the resolutions which he presented to General Davie. But as the Jefferson people were unable to corroborate the date of the Thirty-first Resolves, the Alexander men stood their ground. In the mean time, Martin's History of North Carolina, containing a minute description of what had been done at Charlotte, appeared; but as the controversy had then been raging ten years, Martin's narrative was not accepted.

DECLARATION OF INDEPENDENCE 81

Some years later Martin's preface was examined, and showed that although the book was not printed until 1829, it had in reality been written 1791 to 1809, and finished at least ten years before Mr. Jefferson precipitated the declaration controversy. And a further investigation of Martin's opportunities for ascertaining the truth of what he wrote developed the fact that with the exception of Major Garden, who, in "Anecdotes of the American Revolution," sustains him, Martin is the only historian who personally knew eye-witnesses and participants in the Mecklenburg convention, and had access to the *Cape Fear Mercury* that contained the proceedings of the delegates. And Martin is discredited only by historians writing forty and fifty years after the adoption of the declaration, without any personal knowledge of the events Martin describes.

Our investigations also reveal the fact that Judge Martin's statements are confirmed by the "Mecklenburg Censor" of March 18, 1777, which says the delegates at Charlotte, "the very first, their independence did declare," and sustained by deeds on file in the county court-house dating the time of their execution from the Mecklenburg or "our independence." Martin's version of what was done in May, 1775, is also upheld by Major John Davidson, a signer, whose son, born May 20, 1787, was called by his father My Independence Boy, in honor of the declaration.

If further evidence were needed to corroborate Martin it can be found in the Governor's address to his executive council on June 25, 1775, where he declares the citizens of Mecklenburg County were guilty of "explicitly renouncing obedience to His Majesty's government and all lawful authority whatsoever." Also where that same Governor recites in a proclamation on August 8, 1775, that he has seen in the *Cape Fear Mercury* resolutions, of a committee for the county of Mecklenburg, "declaring the entire dissolution of the laws, government and constitution of this country." And last, James Wallis, a school boy at Sugar Creek Academy, in his declamation on June 1, 1809, reciting the circumstances of the Mecklenburg Declaration, agrees with Martin as to the character of the proceedings on May 19-20, 1775. Thus we find the Mecklenburg resolutions referred to as a Declaration of Independence from the time of their passage in 1775 until 1819, when Mr. Jefferson undertook to invalidate them. All contemporary witnesses, without an exception, testify that the result of the Mecklenburg convention was a Declaration of Independence, and only those writers that appear on the scene a half century after the event declare to the contrary.

Our research further showed that although the Jefferson partizans persistently contend for the authenticity of the Thirty-first Resolves, apparently to protect that statesman from supposed plagiarism, Richard Henry Lee was the author of the phrases common to both declarations. We also discovered that the doubters, while denying the truth of the Mecklenburg Declaration, have never been able to produce one witness testifying to the genuineness of

DECLARATION OF INDEPENDENCE 83

the Resolves of May 31, as printed in the *South Carolina Gazette and County Journal* of June 13, 1775. On the contrary, our examination disclosed the fact that spectators and delegates, the Royal Governor and Martin's History, one and all, declare that resolves embracing the same powers as those of the Thirty-first were enacted by the delegates immediately after adopting the declaration, and this left nothing to be done by the convention on the last day of May. We also learned what became of the *Cape Fear Mercury* containing the proceedings of the delegates, and that the test was not an oath of allegiance to Great Britain, but a test of loyalty to America. And that a signer of the Mecklenburg Declaration of Independence could consistently be a member of the North Carolina Provincial Congress. And, finally, we have found out that there is no doubt of a Declaration of Independence having been made by Mecklenburg County, North Carolina, on May 20, 1775.

THE LIVES OF THE SIGNERS AND A FEW SPECTATORS.

The following sketches of the delegates to the convention at Charlotte are copied almost verbatim from Draper's manuscript work upon the Mecklenburg Declaration of Independence, preserved in the Thwait Library at Madison, Wisconsin:

GEN. THOMAS POLK

The original name of the ancestors of the Polks of Mecklenburg was Muirhead, whence it was changed to Pulloak, then to Pollock—which by obvious transition, assumed its present—as is evident by the will of Magdalene Polk, dated 1723, preserved among the records of the Orphans' Court of Somerset County, Maryland.

The traditions of the Greeks and Romans were not more quaint and curious as to the origin of their heroes than are those of many of the Scotch-Irish Presbyterians who early migrated to the New World. The Polks have had handed down to them a tradition running in this wise:

On a certain great occasion, away back in the misty past, a king of Scotland was marching at the head of an immense procession, when a small oak shrub appeared directly in front of His Majesty, to which one of the king's attendants, by the name of Muirhead, a man of great physical strength, sprang forward, and with a Herculean effort, tore it up by the roots and bore it out of the way. Such an act of gallantry prompted the king to order a halt, when he knighted Muirhead upon the spot, and changed his name to Pulloak—pull-oak. Another tradition is related of the same person. An enormous size and vicious wild boar inhabited that region, a terror to all who came within his range. A reward was offered by the king to any one who would rid the country of the dreaded monster. Pulloak determined to try it single-handed. Armed only with a bow and arrows, he sallied forth on the dangerous adventure. One version of the story is that when the wild boar discovered his pursuer he rushed toward the bold hunter, who climbed an oak tree, and from its branches he shot the fierce animal. Another version of the story is that, pursued by the enraged boar, Pulloak sprang through an old church window, the boar after him; but Pulloak instantly darted out of the door and shut it quickly, and managed to close the window, and then quietly returned home. His neighbors were not a little surprised at his safe return. In response to their expressions of astonishment, he affected equal surprise, saying with nonchalance, truly a bit of a pig had the hardihood to run at him, when he seized it by the tail and threw it into the church window, where they might go and satisfy themselves of the fact. At length some of the more courageous of the number sallied forth to see the game of the forester, and were astonished beyond measure when they discovered the "bit of a pig" was none other than the dreaded wild boar for whose taking off the king had offered the large reward. Some of those present argued that Pulloak was more than a Samson, and must have been imbued with supernatural aid. And as an additional evidence of his fearlessness, he boldly advanced, and shot the enraged animal through one of the windows.

The hero of the exploit, as the tradition goes, kept his own counsel and it was many a long year before he saw fit to divulge the manner of his getting so dangerous a beast into the church alone and single handed. The coat of arms of the Polk family is no doubt derived from the latter tradition—"Polloak, Bar't. Scotch; a boar, passant, pierced by an arrow." Motto: *Audacter et strenne*—Boldly and readily. The boar is represented with elevated bristles and angered mien, transfixed with an arrow.

To aid in ameliorating the natural turbulence of the Irish character, James I encouraged a large emigration into Ireland, and among those who settled in that part of Ulster known as Donnegal was the family of Pollocks. Robert, a son of the elder Pollock, took an active part in the wars against Charles I and fought side by side with Cromwell against the Royalists, under Rupert. The powder horn worn by Robert Pollock during the civil wars is now in possession of Col. W. H. Pollock.

Returning home he married Margarette Tasker the widow of Colonel Porter, and heiress of Mo, a beautiful estate near the town of Giffoard; whose father, Colonel Porter, a chancellor of Ireland, had been an eminent man in his day.

Robert and Magdalene Pollock reared six sons and two daughters. The father and sons obtained grants of land in Maryland from Lord Baltimore. John Pollock, or Polk,—the eldest son,—in 1685 settled at a place called Locust Hammock, in Somerset County, on the eastern shore of Maryland. Thither parents and children migrated at an early period, and became prominent and useful settlers in the colony.

John Polk, who first married —— —— and for his second wife Joanna Knox, died in 1707, leaving two children, William and Nancy.

William, Priscilla, Robert, and Thomas Polk, the subject of this sketch, and the eldest of eight children, was born in Somerset County, Maryland, about 1730. His father moved to the neighborhood of Carlisle, Cumberland County, in 1750, then a newly settled region of Pennsylvania, fast filling up with hardy Scotch-Irish emigrants.

Thomas Polk's early educational advantages must have been quite respectable for that day, since he fitted himself for the occupation of surveyor; and on attaining the age of manhood, and learning of the new settlement along the Catawba Valley, since known as Mecklenburg, he directed his course thither, about the commencement of the border trouble of 1754-'55, the Indian outbreak incited by

French influence extending from the frontiers of New Hampshire to the back settlements of the Carolinas.

Thomas Spratt is said to have been the first man who moved his family on wheels across the Yadkin, stopping a while on Rocky River, and then settling within the present limits of Charlotte. Thomas Polk, when he arrived at Thomas Spratt's, had only a knapsack on his back and a goodly share of indomitable enterprise. He soon married Susanna Spratt, the daughter of this early settler, and their son, William, who distinguished himself in the Revolutionary War, was born in Mecklenburg County in 1758. During the period of 1756 to 1760 there were some Indian troubles on the Catawba and Yadkin frontiers; and it may well be supposed that Thomas Polk here learned some of those lessons of bravery and leadership which he displayed so creditably during the subsequent years of the Revolutionary War. The characteristics of the pioneer settlers of Mecklenburg are well described by an aged native of that region, whose clear memory reaches back into the close of the last century. They were, he says, strong in body, strong in mind, brave and patriotic.

They were driven by persecution from Scotland and Ireland, and were called Scotch-Irish.

They were determined to have *liberty* or have *death*. They lived far from market and had few luxuries. Those who could afford it had coffee for breakfast on Sunday morning, before they went to church, but at no other time. Though they lived plainly, they lived abundantly. The land was rich, producing all manner of grain, stock always plenty and always fat. The women were the best of cooks; no negroes then; no cotton, no drunkards, no thieves; no locks on dwellings, corn-crib or smokehouses. The hardest time of the year was to harvest their crops. Then all through winter they had little to do but to attend their stock, pay and receive visits. Happy days!

Thomas Polk was originally a surveyor, says Dr. Johnson in his traditions of the revolution in the southwestern part of North Carolina; his education was not acquired within the classic walls of a college, but partially obtained at intervals from his occupations in hills, valleys, and forests of the Province.

Then he became universally known and respected, no man possessing more influence in that part of North Carolina. As early as 1770 he was one of the two representatives of Mecklenburg County in the popular house of the Legislature, and in June, 1772, he was employed by Governor Martin as surveyor in running the western extension of the boundary line between North and South Carolina. As indicative of the independent spirit of the people in opposing royal encroachments on their rights, the popular house in February, 1773, refused to vote an appropriation of £172 10s. to pay the claim of the surveyor for running the line, even though so popular a man of the people, and a former member of the house, as Captain Polk, contending that the previous

Assembly had expressed its sense of injury that accrued to the colony by fixing the line as proposed by the Governor.

At the breaking out of the Revolution, Thomas Polk was the colonel of the militia, and the most popular man in Mecklenburg, and all his influence was exerted in behalf of the popular cause.

It is apparent from Martin's History of North Carolina, and from the statements of some of the delegates with reference to the Mecklenburg Resolves of May 20, 1775, that he had the principal agency in calling the convention of which he was a conspicuous member and popular leader of the people. Foote says that he was well known and well acquainted in the surrounding counties, a man of great excellence and merited popularity. He was also one of the Mecklenburg members of the Provincial Congress that held sessions at Hillsborough during August and September, 1775, and served on important committees—one to prepare a plan for the regulation of internal peace, order and safety of the Province. On September 9, 1775, he was appointed by the Provincial Congress colonel of the militia of Mecklenburg, and in November and December following, marched at the head of six companies, aggregating three hundred men, into the southeastern part of South Carolina to aid in suppressing an outbreak of the Tories in that quarter. Some 300 pounds of powder was supplied by the authorities of North Carolina for the use of his troops against the insurgents near Ninety-Six. It was a hard service with some fighting. The Tories were subdued and many

DECLARATION OF INDEPENDENCE 91

made prisoners, and in consequence of a heavy snow fall, it was called the snow campaign. This service was all the more creditable since it was to serve a neighboring Province in suppressing a dangerous insurrection, and Colonel Richardson, the South Carolina commander, was directed to take Colonel Polk's men into the pay of the colony for the expedition, and tender them the thanks of the South Carolina Council of Safety, with the assurance that "the service of those good neighbors" would ever be held in grateful remembrance.

In December, while absent on this service, he was appointed colonel of the Second of the two regiments of Minute Men, ordered to be raised in the district of Salisbury, composed of Rowan, Mecklenburg, Tryon and Surry counties. He had been but a brief period returned from South Carolina when he was called to lead his regiment against the Tory Highlanders on the Cape Fear in February, 1776, and reaching Cross Creek, now Fayetteville, received intelligence of the decisive victory of Caswell and Lillington over the insurgents, and returned home.

In April he was recommended by the Provincial Congress to the command of the Fourth of the six Continental regiments, which the Continental Congress confirmed early in May; and the same month he was ordered with his regiment to join General Moore at Cape Fear. The six Continental regiments finally rendezvoused at Wilmington, from which at least a portion were ordered in June to the defense of Charleston, Polk's regiment being of the number. But a single regiment of the North Carolinians, Clarke's, appears to have had any active part in repelling the enemy from Charleston. This service ended, the North Carolina Continentals seem to have returned to their old camp at Wilmington, and drilled and perfected themselves during the summer and autumn, when they were marched into South Carolina.

In February, 1777, Francis Nash, who had just been promoted to a brigadier, was ordered by the Continental Congress to use his influence in the western part of North Carolina to stimulate the filling up of the Continental regiments, and march the ensuing month to join General Washington.

Maj. William Lee Davidson, of Polk's regiment, marched with the North Carolina line, but it is not apparent that Colonel Polk himself engaged in the service. It is probable that inasmuch as the Continental regiments were deficient in numbers, there were only enough of Polk's to form a major's command.

From this time to the fall of Charleston, in May, 1780, was comparatively a quiet period in North Carolina.

In 1777 Liberty Hall Academy was established in Charlotte on grounds and improvements purchased by Colonel Polk, and he was made one of the trustees. Thus were means for public education provided and sustained, until the institution was suspended by the subsequent British invasion of the country. In 1780 Colonel Polk had troops at Charlotte guarding the public magazines, which were removed when the enemy approached in September of the same year. He acted as commissary-general of supplies both for the North Carolina troops and the Continentals under General Yates (Lee Paper, N. Y. Hist. Society, p. 145), and there was some complaint for inattention to duty on his part in his important office, which he explained upon the ground of scarcity of supplies and necessary attention to his family.

Col. Alexander Martin, a member of the State Board of War, to which Colonel Polk was amenable, having visited the army of Mecklenburg, declares in a public letter recorded in the journal of the board, that in his opinion Colonel Polk had fulfilled the duties of his office as well as circumstances would admit.

During Cornwallis's occupancy of the country, Colonel Polk had necessarily to retire from Charlotte, and his residence became the headquarters of the British general. An original letter written by him at this period to the North Carolina Board of War is in possession of Col. J. H. Wheeler, viz.:

"CAMP YADKIN RIVER, Oct. 11, 1780.

"GENTLEMEN:—I have the pleasure to inform you that on Saturday last the noted Colonel Ferguson, with 150 men, fell on King's Mountain; 800 taken prisoners, with 150 stand of arms. Cleveland and Campbell commanded. Glorious affair. In a few days doubt not we shall be in Charlotte, and I will take possession of my house and *his* lordship take the woods.

"I am, gentlemen, with respect,
"Your humble servant,
"THOMAS POLK."

How such a man as Colonel Polk should have been under a cloud of distrust even for a short time, as Lossing states, is a little marvelous; yet some mischief-making person must have invented a "suspicion that he had accepted of protection from the British," and reported it to Gates, who returned from his late defeat, and the recent treachery of Arnold, readily surmised "suspicious circumstances," and ordered Colonel Polk to Salisbury to answer for his conduct. So utterly baseless were those cruel suspicions that they were promptly dismissed, and Colonel Polk was continued in his double office of commissary-general of provisions for the State of North Carolina and commissary of purchases for the Continental troops. The very first night that General Greene, having succeeded Gates, passed at headquarters early in December, he spent with Colonel Polk in studying the resources of the country, and by "the following morning," said Polk to Elkanah Watson, "he better understood them than Gates had done during the whole period of his command." The Mecklenburg region had been the granary of provisions for the Americans for the whole season, and for the British for a short season, the latter demanding heavy supplies; according to Stedman, their commissary-general demanding 100 cattle per day.

The country was, therefore, so much exhausted that Colonel Polk, who still acted as commissary from patriotic motives, declared that it could scarcely afford subsistence for a single week. It was with regret that General Greene learned from him that many reasons conspired, rendering it necessary for him to relinquish the office. "I am now too far advanced in years to undergo the task and fatigue of a commissary-general," wrote Polk to Greene on December 10th. On the same day Greene wrote to Col. William R. Davie, inviting him to that position, saying, "Colonel Polk finds the business of subsisting the army too laborious and difficult for him to conduct, and, therefore, has sent in his resignation to the Board of War, but the greatest difficulty with him is, he cannot leave home owing to the peculiar state of his family." Dr. Johnson has presented in his traditions of the Revolution the following letter:

"CAMP CHARLOTTE, Dec. 15, 1780.
"*To Colonel Polk:*

"SIR:—I find it will be impossible to leave camp as early as I intended, as Colonel Kascius has made no report respecting a position upon Pee Dee. I must, therefore, beg you to continue the daily supplies of the army, and keep in readiness three days' provisions beforehand. I have just received some intelligence from Governor Nash and from Congress which makes me wish to see you.   I am, etc

"NATHAN GREENE."

There is proof that General Greene had such unlimited confidence in Colonel Polk that he wished to confide in him intelligence that he did not wish to write. Before retiring from service, on General Greene's appeal, he exerted himself to procure lumber for the barracks at the new position selected for the army on Hicks's Creek nearly opposite Cheraw Hill, on the Pee Dee; to build boats for the transportation of stores; to collect provisions, and do everything that could be done to enable the new commander to prepare his men for the active duties of the coming campaign.

General Greene's letters evince a high appreciation of Colonel Polk's service, and a still higher evidence of his confidence in his skill and patriotism may be found in the fact that upon the fall of the gallant General Davidson, early in February, 1781, Greene appointed Polk to fill the vacancy on the recommendation of the officers of the brigade as the fittest person for the important position among all the many patriotic soldiers of Mecklenburg.

On the receipt of the news of the battle of Guilford, it was thought Cornwallis would retrace his steps by the way of Salisbury and Charlotte, so as to keep open the communication and act in concert with Lord Rowdon at Camden; and as the citizens of that section had already experienced the distress of the presence of the British soldiers, they determined to do their best to keep the enemy at a distance. General Polk accordingly ordered out the next division of militia liable for duty, with a view of marching to Salisbury to fortify the fords and passes on the Yadkin, but before reaching there intelligence was received that the British were directing their course toward Fayetteville, when Colonel Polk dismissed his men and returned.

General Greene re-entered South Carolina in April, taking position before Camden. He called upon North Carolina for a draft of three months' men, when Colonel Polk exerted himself to meet the demands of the occasion, and led a considerable force of his countrymen, and joined Greene at Rugeley's Mills shortly after the battle at Hobkirk's Hill, and remained in that border region, watching and checking the British and Tories in both Carolinas, until the expiration of the term of service for which his men had been drafted. This appears to have been Colonel Polk's last military service. Governor Graham well observes that when placed in command as brigadier-general, "in all after, as in prior times, he was regarded as an unwavering patriot."

General Polk now retired to private life, which, with his advancing years, he yearned to enjoy. After Rutherford's expedition in the autumn of 1781, in pursuit of a body of Tories under McNeil and other Tory leaders, peace was practically restored in North Carolina.

He owned mills two miles south of Charlotte, and kept a store in the village, and was now enabled to give his undivided time to his private affairs.

Elkanah Watson, in his "Men and Times of the Revolution," who visited Charlotte in 1785, states "I carried letters to the courteous General Polk, and remained two days at his residence in the delightfu society of his charming family."

After the war, when the disbanded soldiers o: the North Carolina line received their land warrants in payment for their military services, General Polk purchased many of these warrants and went, early in 1786, with his four sons, armed with their rifles into the wilderness of Duck River County, in Middle Tennessee, to locate them, Col. William Polk having been chosen in 1793 one of the principal surveyors Resuming his original profession of surveyor, Gen eral Polk selected the finest lands in that rich valley ran the line, marked them, and secured the titles notwithstanding the hostility of the Indians. S when he died in 1793, he left a rich inheritance i lands for his children. "He was," says Dr. J. C Ramsey, "a high-souled cavalier, full of dash an courage; rich, hospitable, and charming." Dr. John son relates that several of his children were wild an frolicsome—one bore the sobriquet of "Dev Charley"; that on one occasion the General wa speaking of the boldness of single highway robbery and declared that no single man would dare mak such an attempt on him. The sons all heard it, an Charley resolved to have his fun, even at his father expense. So when his father was returning on by-road with a sum of money he had been collecting, the reckless son, disguised, waylaid him in a creek bottom and demanded the instant delivery of his money. The General's first thought was to snatch up his pistols, but Charles was too quick for him, and seeing a pistol, as he supposed, presented at his breast, the father gave up his money and returned home not a little fretted and mortified at the result. Perceiving his depression of spirits, the young men inquired into the cause and offered their aid in any difficulties. He frankly told them he had been robbed of such a sum of money, designating the place. They all expressed surprise, and inquired if he were not armed. He acknowledged that he had his pistols, but had not had time to use them. When they concluded that there must have been several highwaymen banded together to have effected their purpose, he, with increased mortification, confessed that there was but one; but added that he was off his guard, and was taken by surprise. Charles at this point returned the money, acknowledging that he had taken it from him. "What!" exclaimed the General, "Did you endanger your father's life?" "No, sir," said Charles. "What, did you not present a pistol at my breast?" "No, sir," replied the son. "How can you say that?" asked the father. "I assure you, sir, it was only my mother's brass candlestick that I took off from your own mantelpiece."

Of Colonel Polk's three daughters, Margaret married Dr. Ephraim Brevard, whose name is so intimately associated with the Mecklenburg Convention and famous Resolves of May 20, 1775. She died early and left an only daughter, Margaret Polk, who became the wife of Nathaniel Alexander, a native of Mecklenburg, who graduated at Princeton in 1776, and after studying medicine, entered the army, served in the House of Commons in 1797, in the State Senate in 1801 and 1802, and, while holding a seat in Congress in 1803-05, he was chosen by the Legislature Governor of the State, serving two years. He died at Charlotte, November 8, 1808, at the age of 52 years, leaving no children. General Polk's third daughter married a man named Brown, leaving no issue.

COL. ABRAHAM ALEXANDER

The Alexanders were very numerous at the time of the Revolution and since in Mecklenburg, and although of the same original Scotch-Irish stock, they were of different degrees of consanguinity Hezekiah and John McKnitt Alexander were brothers; while Abraham, Adam, Charles and Ezra Alexander were their cousins. (See Mans. Letters of Dr. J. G. M. Ramsay, October 2, 1875.)

Foote relates that, among Presbyterian emigrations from Scotland to Ireland, to escape persecution for conscience's sake, during the period between 1610 and 1688, there were seven brothers bearing the same name of Alexander.

But their grievances increasing a few years preceding the Revolution of 1688, their minister imprisoned for holding fasts, the Alexanders resolved to seek quiet and repose in the New World

On the eve of their departure, they sent to Scotland for their old preacher to baptize their children and administer to them the consolations of the Gospel. The faithful and fearless preacher arrived in time to meet the friends on the vessel on which they had embarked, and there held becoming religious services. An armed company now came on board, broke up the meeting, and lodged the minister in jail. Toward night an old matron addressed her kinsman: "Men, gang ye away, tak' our minister out o' the jail, and tak' him, guide soule, wi' us till Ameriky." Her commands had never been disobeyed. Before morning the minister was on board and the vessel had proceeded on its voyage. The minister having no family, cheerfully consented to the arrangement, and with joy and thanksgiving they landed safely on Manhattan. Part of the company remained there, from whom it is related Wm. Alexander, commonly known as Lord Sterling, a major-general of the Revolution, descended. The others took up their abode for a time in New Jersey; then settled in part, perhaps, in Cecil County, Maryland, and others in Pennsylvania. There they mingled with their countrymen, intermarried, and their descendants in great numbers migrated to the Catawba country, following the great valley of Virginia from Pennsylvania and Maryland. This movement began slowly about 1745, and more rapidly from 1750 onward. Maj. Thomas Alexander and Dan Alexander, both soldiers of the Revolution, were natives of Mecklenburg, the former having been born in 1753, the latter in 1758. Abraham Alexander was among those early emigrants. He was born, apparently, in Cecil County, Maryland, in 1717, and migrated early to the Catawba country; soon attained a prominent position among the pioneer settlers. He was long a leading magistrate of his county, and the honored chairman of the Inferior Court both before and during the Revolution. With Col. Thomas Polk, he represented Mecklenburg in the Assembly in 1771, and ranked among the leading Whigs of that day. He seemed, however, not to have been ambitious for honor and place, for he declined at the next election to solicit the suffrage of the people. He is next found presiding at the Mecklenburg Convention of May 20, 1775, and was active during the whole period of the Revolution, both as member of the Justice Court and as chairman of the Committee of Safety. He was, in 1777, appointed as one of the original trustees of Liberty Hall Academy, and was for many years an elder in Sugar Creek Presbyterian Church. He died April 28, 1778, in the 69th year of his age, and his widow, Dorcas, survived till May 28th, when she passed away in her 67th year, and her remains rest beside those of her husband in the old Sugar Creek burial ground. They had five sons and one daughter—Abraham, Isaac, Nathaniel, Elias, and Joab. Isaac became a distinguished physician, and settled in Camden, S. C., while his brothers spent their days as tillers of the soil. Elizabeth, the sister, became the wife of William Alexander, son of Hezekiah Alexander.

DR. EPHRAIM BREVARD

The earliest known Brevard was a French Huguenot, leaving his native land on the revocation of the Edict of Nantes, and settling among the Scotch-Irish in the northern part of Ireland, where he formed an acquaintance with a family of McKnitts, in company with whom he sailed for America. Among the McKnitt emigrants was a blooming lassie, who may have had quite as much to do in attracting his attention as the cheap lands and glowing accounts of the New World. A mutual attachment sprang up, which eventuated in marriage. They settled on the waters of Elk River, Cecil County, in the northeastern corner of Maryland, bordering on Pennsylvania. Five sons and one daughter were the issue of this union, of whom John, Robert, Zebulon, and their married sister and husband migrated to the Yadkin and Catawba country about 1747, and settled in what was subsequently Rowan, and since Iredell County.

Some years prior to this removal, John Brevard, the elder of the brothers, had married Jane McWhirter, a sister of Dr. Alex McWhirter, of Scotch-Irish extraction, of the adjoining county of New Castle, Delaware; and their fifth child and eldest son, Ephraim, was born in 1744 in Cecil County, Maryland, and was only about three years old when his parents removed to the wilds of North Carolina, settling in what subsequently became Iredell County. While a boy he had the misfortune to lose one of his eyes, and after attending a classical school near his father's residence, he was sent, on the conclusion of the Indian war in 1761, with his cousin, Adlai Osborne, to attend a grammar school in Prince Edward County, Virginia, under William Capples. The young men, with Thomas Reese, entered Princeton College in 1766, graduating in 1768. Reese and Brevard taught school some time in Maryland, which enabled Brevard to put himself under the tuition of Dr. David Ramsay, subsequently so celebrated in civil life during the Revolution and as an historian after the war. After pursuing his medical studies some time in Philadelphia, Dr. Ramsay removed to Somerset County, Maryland. Brevard accompanied him, and after a due course there, he commenced the practice of his profession in Charlotte. Possessed of more than common abilities, well cultured under the instructions of Dr. Witherspoon, Dr. Ramsay and others, and of prepossessing manners, he at once took a prominent position and exerted a large influence among the Mecklenburg people. He was soon united in marriage with a daughter of Col. Thomas Polk, who died leaving him an only daughter. The distinguished part he acted in the Mecklenburg Convention of May 20, 1775, as a member, and the reputed author of the Mecklenburg Declaration of Independence Resolves of May 20, 1775, will cause his name to ever fill an honored place in the record of western Carolina. Bancroft declares that his name "should be remembered with honor by his countrymen" for having "digested the system which was then adopted and formed in effect a Declaration of Independence, as well as a complete system of government," and Gridsby pronounces him an exalted patriot, and as to the record of the Resolves, that the beauty of their diction, their elegant precision, the wide scope of statesmanship which they exhibit, prove incontestibly that the man who put them forth was worthy of their high trust at the difficult crisis.

In February, 1776, we find him the tutor of the Queen's Museum Academy, with nineteen young men under him, whom he led as their captain in Colonel Polk's regiment in an expedition against Scotch Tories on the Cape Fear. How long he continued teaching is not known.

In 1777, when Liberty Hall Academy was organized, he was one of the original trustees, and his name as such is appended to a degree given to John Graham in 1778.

After performing every duty to his people befitting a patriot, he entered the Southern army as a surgeon, and was captured at the surrender of Charleston in May, 1780. There, from long confinement and unwholesome diet, he was taken sick, and when at length set at liberty, he reached the home of his friend, John McKnitt Alexander, where he lingered for several months, his disease baffling the best medical skill—Dr. William Read, Physician General to the Southern army, visiting him from the hospital at Charlotte. He finally breathed his last some time in 1781, about the age of 37 years, and was probably buried in Hopewell Cemetery near John McKnitt Alexander's home, although tradition says he is interred in Charlotte on the square now occupied by the county court-house, and bounded by Third, Fourth, Tryon, and College streets. Before and during the Revolutionary War Queen's Museum, afterwards called Liberty Hall, established in 1771, by the Mecklenburg Presbyterians in opposition to British authority, stood on this ground. And when Cornwallis occupied Charlotte with his army in September and October, 1780, the buildings were used for a hospital, and the soldiers that died there were buried near the house. Consequently, it is not reasonable to suppose under those circumstances, that John McKnitt Alexander, with his church, Hopewell, near at hand, would bring the remains of Brevard nine miles to Charlotte, where there was no church in that day, and bury them among British soldiers whose government was still waging war on the American colonies.

In the language of Dr. Foote, "He thought clearly, felt deeply, wrote well, resisted bravely, and died a martyr to that liberty none loved better and few understood so well." He was a man of undoubted genius and talent. (See MS. Letters of Rev. R. H. King to Dr. J. G. M. Ramsay, April 9, 1823.) His only daughter, on arriving at years of womanhood, married a Dickerson, settled at Camden, S. C., and left one child, a son, James Polk Dickerson, who was lieutenant-colonel of Butler's regiment of South Carolina Volunteers in the Mexican war; was severely wounded at the siege of Vera Cruz March 11, 1847; recovering from that, he was again badly

Declaration of Independence

wounded at Cherubusco on the 20th of August following, and died of his wound three weeks later, greatly regretted by his regiment and the whole army.

COL. ADAM ALEXANDER

The place of Col. A. Alexander's birth is not certainly known, but he was possibly a native of Cecil County, Maryland, and was born in 1728. He was among the pioneer settlers of Mecklenburg. He married a Miss Shelby. As early as June, 1770, we find him a prominent member of Clear Creek congregation, and the next year he commanded a company under General Waddell to aid in putting down the Regulators, who had taken the law in their own hands in upholding the usurpations and extortions of Governor Tryon's favorites. That Captain Alexander was unwilling to shed the blood of his oppressed countrymen is readily seen by the course he and other officers pursued in persuading Waddell to return from their camp on Pott's Creek across the Yadkin, both on account of the superiority of the insurgents, and the unwillingness of the men to engage them, while waiting for a convoy of ammunition under a small guard from Charlotte. A party of ten or twelve, under Capt. William Alexander, blackened and disguised, seized the convoy and destroyed the powder, and ever after he was known as "Black Billy" Alexander.

Capt. Adam Alexander, on the day of the 11th of May, immediately after uniting with his brother officers in advising a retreat beyond the Yadkin, went in person and reconnoitered the Regulators, and returning, reported that he had passed along their lines and the footmen appeared to him to extend a quarter of a mile, seven or eight deep, and that the horsemen, 120 yards, twelve or fourteen deep. On the 19th Waddell, with his small force of 250 men, was obliged to retreat from his position, two miles eastward of the Yadkin, to Salisbury, the Regulators having surrounded his party and threatened to cut them to pieces if they offered to join the main army under Tryon. But the principal body of the insurgents had been defeated on the 16th at Alamance, and Tryon marched with his victorious troops to join Waddell, then entrenched near Salisbury, eight miles to the eastward of the Yadkin. Receiving intelligence that the Regulators in the region embracing the present counties of Mecklenburg, Lincoln, and Iredell were meditating further hostilities, General Waddell was sent into that quarter with a strong detachment, including the Mecklenburg troops. Early in June, with orders, after he had performed the service assigned him, to disband his troops, meeting with no opposition, he had little to do besides administering the oath of allegiance to the people. Adam Alexander was many years a prominent magistrate and member of the County Court, and on May 20, 1775, was one of the members of the Mecklenburg Convention. In September following, he was appointed lieutenant-colonel of the Mecklenburg "Minute Men" under Colonel Polk, and served shortly after in one of the Snow Campaigns against the Tories in South Carolina.

When the "Minute Men" of the Salisbury district were, in December, 1775, formed into two groups, he was re-appointed lieutenant-colonel of the Second Regiment under Colonel Polk, and marched, in February, 1776, to aid in quelling the insurrection of the Highlanders on the Cape Fear.

In the ensuing April, when Polk was chosen to command one of the Continental regiments, Adam Alexander succeeded him as colonel of the Mecklenburg regiments. When the Cherokees commenced hostilities early in the summer of 1776, incited thereto by the machinations of the enemy, Colonel Alexander led a force to the head of the Catawba, where he served six weeks in protecting the Catawba Valley during the harvest, and went with his regiment under General Rutherford, later in the season, on his expedition against the treacherous Cherokees, destroying their crops and villages.

Dr. Caldwell refers to Colonel Alexander when President Washington made his Southern tour in 1792, as "far advanced in life." His death occurred in 1798, at the age of 70 years, lamented by all who knew him. His remains were interred at Rock Springs. Adam Alexander was a man of military genius, remarkably endowed. He was a Presbyterian.

He had four sons—Evan, Isaac, Adam, and Charles, and one daughter, Mary. She married John Springs. All the Springs of Mecklenburg, a large, wealthy and intelligent connection, are descendants of Colonel Alexander.

His son, Evan Alexander, whom he sent to Princeton with the hope that he would enter the ministry, graduated in 1787, became a prominent lawyer in Charlotte; was two years a member of the Legislature, then representative in Congress from 1805 to 1809, and died unmarried October 28th, in the latter year.

Isaac Alexander held various offices of trust in the county, while his brother Charles occupied the old homestead, married a Miss Means, and had several talented sons, who died young.

GEN. ROBERT IRWIN

William Irwin was one of the early Scotch-Irish settlers in West Pennsborough, Cumberland County, Pennsylvania, a few miles southeast of Carlisle. His son, Robert, the eighth of thirteen children, was born August 26, 1740, and was reared with few advantages on his native homestead. When his father died, not long prior to May, 1763, the farm of one hundred acres was purchased of the heirs at £15 each, by their elder brother, John Irwin, and with this Robert Irwin commenced life and wended his way to the Steele Creek settlement in Mecklenburg. He was soon after united in marriage with Mary Alexander, daughter of Zebulon Alexander, an early emigrant from Pennsylvania. About the period of 1767, Robert Irwin was one of the first bench of elders of Steele Creek Church. He was one of the members of the Mecklenburg Convention in May, 1775, and thenceforward proved himself one of the active leaders of the Mecklenburg people during the war. It is altogether probable he had seen service during the French and Indian War on the frontier of Pennsylvania, for Colonel Armstrong led many a daring force against the Indians during that period from the Carlisle region; and more probably still he was employed against the Regulators in 1771, and on the Snow Campaign near the close of 1775. After having served as a member of the North Carolina Provincial Congress in April and May, 1776, he engaged in General Rutherford's campaign against the Cherokees during the summer and autumn of that year. Returning from this expedition in October, he was rechosen to a seat in the Provincial Congress, which met in November in the double capacity of making laws and forming a new Constitution. On the death of Lieutenant-Colonel Phifer, he succeeded him in 1777 as second in command of the Mecklenburg militia.

General Irwin died at his residence in the Steele Creek settlement, in Mecklenburg County, December 23, 1800, in his 61st year, and was interred in the Steele Creek burial ground, his wife's remains occupying the same grave. On his tombstone is engraved this beautiful and truthful delineation of his character, "Great, noble, generous, good and brave."

JOHN M'KNITT ALEXANDER

Little more can be said of Mr. Alexander than has already been indicated. Born in 1733, in Pennsylvania, as stated by Dr. Foote, but according to more reliable information, in the northeastern portion of Cecil County, Maryland, where his father, James

Alexander, settled on a tract of land called New Munster, in 1714, where soon after he married Margaret McKnitt, a sister of John McKnitt, an early emigrant to the southern part of the same county. The father, James Alexander, remained in Maryland, surviving till 1779; but his son, John McKnitt Alexander, who had served an apprenticeship to a tailor, migrated in 1754, when 21 years old, to Mecklenburg County, accompanied by his brother, Hezekiah, and sister, Jemima, and her husband, Maj. Thomas Sharpe, also of Cecil County. In the early days of Mecklenburg, when the deer and buffalo furnished not only viands for the table, but a portion of apparel for the people, a leather-breeches maker was not probably a sufficiently profitable occupation for the enterprising young Marylander; so we soon find him a land surveyor and a large land-holder, surveying and taking lands as far away as Chester District, in South Carolina, forty miles distant. In 1759 he married Jane Bane, from Pennsylvania, of the same Scotch-Irish stock with himself, and settled in the Hopewell congregation. Enterprising, shrewd, and honorable, he prospered in business and became wealthy. Colonel Wheeler, in his "Sketches of Mecklenburg Delegates," states that Mr. Alexander was a member of the Provincial Assembly in 1772, while Jones's defense indicates that Martin Phifer and John Davidson were the Mecklenburg representatives at that time. But his was a busy and useful life in the civil time, during the Revolutionary War, long and faithfully serving as a magistrate and member of the County Court;

one of the members of the Mecklenburg Convention of May 20, 1775; the successor of Dr. Brevard as secretary of the Mecklenburg Committee of Safety, and a representative in the Provincial Congress in August and September, 1775. The same year he visited Philadelphia, where he communicated to Dr. Franklin the facts and circumstances of the preceding Mecklenburg Convention, when they were fresh in his memory, who expressed his approbation of their act. In April, 1776, we again find him a member of the Provincial Congress; in the State Senate in 1777, and the same year chosen a trustee of Liberty Hall Academy.

How Mr. Alexander regarded the Red Coats when they invaded the soil of Mecklenburg in the fall of 1780, may best be seen in the notice of Duncan Ochiltree. It was a high compliment to his sterling patriotism that General Davidson, at that period, named his encampment in Mecklenburg "Camp McKnitt Alexander."

When Cornwallis undertook the vain effort of endeavoring to recover the Cowpens prisoners from Morgan, early in 1781, and General Greene exerted himself to thwart his Lordship's purpose, Mr. Alexander, though his age would have excused him from exposure, accompanied Greene as a pilot, if not a volunteer aid, and was actively employed in destroying, or sinking, ferry boats on the Yadkin and Dan rivers; and by his zeal in the cause, his intimate knowledge as an old surveyor of the topography of the roads, and people of the county, he was able to afford valuable assistance as counsellor to the American general.

For many years he was a sturdy Presbyterian, an elder in the church, and a prominent actor in all its public convocations. During the closing five or six years of his life he was nearly blind and very infirm; but his children, grand-children, and numerous friends loved and revered him, and united in lamenting his separation from them July 10, 1817, in the 85th year of his age. In the graveyard at Hopewell his remains sleep in peace beside those of his beloved companion. He left two sons, William Bane and Dr. Joseph McKnitt Alexander; and of his five daughters, one, Abigail Bane, was united in marriage to Rev. S. C. Caldwell; another to Rev. James Wallis, and a third to Col. Francis A. Ramsay, father of the worthy historian of Tennessee. As he appeared to D. G. Stinson in 1813, Mr. Alexander was a man of medium size, dark skin, with a good intellectual face, neat and tidy in his dress; he was very dignified, and had the reputation of being a very sensible person. He was quite a politician in his day, of the old Federal school—while his son-in-law, Rev. James Wallis, was a prominent Democratic leader, and was often engaged to deliver political addresses on the Fourth of July occasions

REV. HEZEKIAH BALCH

The Balch family was originally from Wales, and the name signifies "proud" in the Welsh language. John Balch is said to have emigrated to New

England at an early period from Bridgewater, in Somerset, England, and became possessed of a large property and extensive influence. A great grandson of his, Col. James Balch, migrated directly from his native England, married Anne Goodwine, and settled on Deer Creek, in Harford County, Maryland, where his eldest son, Hezekiah, was born in 1746. His father was a man of highly gifted and cultivated mind, possessing a fine poetical talent, and was the author of some anonymous pieces that had no small celebrity in their day. While his son was yet a youth, the father moved with his family from Maryland and settled in Mecklenburg.

After assisting his father on the farm, young Balch was at length sent to Princeton College, where he graduated in 1766 in the same class with Waightstill Avery, Chief Justice Ellsworth, and the celebrated Luther Martin. He was licensed to preach by the Presbytery of Donnegal in 1767, and in 1769 he was ordained and sent as a missionary to Rocky River and Poplar Tent churches, within the limits of Mecklenburg. He had married (a Miss Sconnel, it is believed) shortly before removing to the county, and settled six miles west of the present town of Concord, on the Beattie's Ford road. It must be conceded that during his brief period of labor, about seven years, he performed a good pioneer work for the Church and State—for the cause of liberty and the cause of education. A member of the Mecklenburg Convention of May, 1775, he not only voted for the noble Resolves, but enforced them by his vigorous sense and eloquence. He did what he could for his country and his kind; but in the summer of 1776 he was called to his reward at the early age of 30 years. He was reputed an elegant and accomplished scholar. He is said to have been a tall, handsome man, with fair hair, which he wore long and curling. He had two or more children. His widow subsequently married a man by the name of McWhorter, a professional teacher, and moved with him and her children to Tennessee, Mrs. McWhorter taking the children as she passed along on her journey to view their father's grave for the last time. All trace of these children has been lost. Mr. Balch had three brothers and several sisters. Two of the former were noted Presbyterian clergymen, Rev. Dr Steven B. Balch, of Georgetown, and Rev. James Balch, of Kentucky; the third, William Balch, a planter in Georgia. In 1847 means were provided and a suitable monument erected over his grave, for which Rev. J. A. Wallace prepared an appropriate inscription.

HEZEKIAH ALEXANDER

This member of the numerous Alexander family was a brother of John McKnitt Alexander, and was born in Cecil County, in the northern part of Maryland, in January, 1722. He migrated with his family to the Mecklenburg country in 1754, and was soon assigned a prominent place among the early settlers. He located four or five miles east of Charlotte and in 1764 erected a stone residence on which the date is cut, and is a good house to this day. He was for many years a magistrate and member of the County Court. Foote relates of him that he was "the clearest-headed magistrate in the county," a high compliment. In May, 1775, he served in the Mecklenburg Convention, and in the ensuing September he was chosen a member of the Salisbury District Committee of Safety. In April, 1776, he was appointed paymaster of Col. Thomas Polk's regiment of the Continentals, and the next month he was chosen one of the two members to represent the Salisbury District in the State Council of Safety, on pay of twenty shillings proclamation money for each day's traveling and attendance. He died June 16, 1801.

CAPT. ZACCHEUS WILSON

The Wilsons were of Scotch-Irish Presbyterian stock, and were among the early settlers of Cumberland County, Pennsylvania, where Zaccheus Wilson was born, probably as early as about 1735 or 1740. When he grew to man's estate, he was not "little of statue" as Zaccheus of old—for like nearly all of that numerous connection, his person was of full medium size, rather heavily framed, and possessing great power in the vigor of life. He received but a limited education, and while yet quite young settled with his parents in the Poplar Tent region, originally a part of Mecklenburg, now Cabarrus County. This was prior to March, 1753. He had a younger sister who married Capt. Stephen Alexander, who survived till the age of 90—the chronicler of her region.

Zaccheus Wilson had three brothers, two of whom were Robert and David, and three sisters. Reared on the frontier, Zaccheus and his brothers were not the men to have shirked any duty in aiding in the defence of the country. On the Yadkin River, in Rowan County, one Nicholas Ross early settled, marrying Lizzie Conger, daughter of John Conger. There were then many wild horses running in the woods. Having a fine animal of his own, and needing another, Ross went in the spring of the year to the range and selected one that he thought would suit his purpose, and started to run him down and halter him. But in the race, the horse plunged in a hole, turned a complete somersault, and fell back on and crushed his pursuer, who left a widow and two little daughters. (MS. Letter of Rev. Nicholson Ross Morgan, a son of the younger of Mr. Ross's daughters. The elder married Matthew Harris, a nephew of Col. Robert and Samuel Harris, of Rocky River.)

Zaccheus Wilson, in his occupation of a surveyor, was sent for to survey and divide the land for the heirs; saw, admired, and married the young widow, and took her to his home in the Steele Creek region.

About 1767, we find him one of the elders of Steele Creek Church. He had a decided love for mathematical studies, which he pursued with little or no instruction, and became one of the best surveyors of his day.

He was a member of the Mecklenburg Convention in May, 1775, and of the Provincial Congress of November, 1776, for making laws and forming a

Constitution. The only military service particularly remembered, though much in the army, was as a Captain at King's Mountain, where among plunder taken was an English surveyor's compass and platting instruments, which were assigned to him in the division, and are yet preserved by one of his descendants. He was a member of the North Carolina Convention of 1788 for the consideration of the Federal Constitution, and he was among the large majority that refused to give it their approval, as wanting in a proper protection of the rights of the people.

When the county of Cabarrus was set off from Mecklenburg, in 1792, Captain Wilson was a resident of that region, and was chosen county surveyor.

In 1796, Captain Wilson, having lost his wife, resolved on following his brother, Maj. David Wilson, who had nine years before moved to Sumner County, Tennessee; and just prior to his departure he visited his step-daughter, the mother of the venerable Rev. N. H. Morgan. "The last night he spent with us," says Mr. Morgan, "I slept with him, and about midnight the wolves raised a furious howling around the cow pen. The old gentleman went out and chased them away, and I as a mere lad remember how I trembled lest he should be devoured." In this migration, besides his two sons, a goodly number of Wilsons and some Alexanders accompanied him. His removal was much regretted by his old friends and neighbors. His education, mostly self-acquired, was quite liberal. He was very popular, a Presbyterian spotless in life, a noble, worthy man, without an equal in his profession as a surveyor. He settled one mile northeast of Gallatin, in Sumner County, twenty-six miles above Nashville, where he followed his profession as long as he was able to do so. He died in 1824.

NEIL MORRISON

James Morrison, a native of Scotland, early migrated to this country; settled in Philadelphia, where his son, Neil Morrison, was born in 1728. On reaching years of manhood, he engaged in mercantile business in that city, and then married.

A few years before the Revolution the father and his three sons moved to Mecklenburg and located on Four Mile Creek, in Providence settlement, Neil Morrison at this time having a family. James Morrison lived to be an old man of 81 years, and was interred in Providence burial ground. Neil Morrison's abilities soon commanded respect, and he was chosen one of the members of the Mecklenburg Convention in May, 1775. He engaged heartily in the military service, commanding a company on Rutherford's campaign in 1776, against the Cherokee Indians, burning their towns, cutting down their corn and throwing it into the streams.

His other services are not known. He was a justice of the peace and a member of the County Court. He died September 13, 1784, at the age of 56 years, and was buried in Providence graveyard. His widow survived him until her 89th year. His son, William Morrison, was early sent to Princeton

College, but the war early in 1776 interrupted his studies, so he bought himself a rifle and returned home, and entered the service, serving a while on Sullivan's Island. At Gates's defeat in August, 1780, he was wounded by a musket ball, taken prisoner and confined in jail in Camden, whence his mother and sister succeeded in getting him pardoned; then conveyed him to Charlotte, where Dr. Henderson extracted the ball and he recovered. He subsequently became a prominent physician, and died in 1806, together with his brothers, Alexander and James, all within a period of three months. Dr. William Morrison was a member of the Legislature in 1796—elected as a Federalist—and his brother, Alexander, in 1801 to 1803, as a Republican. Their sister became the wife of Maj. Thomas Alexander, who served under Davie and Sumter in the Revolution.

RICHARD BARRY

Of Scotch-Irish descent, Richard Barry was born in Pennsylvania in 1726. He married Anne Price, of Maryland, also of Scotch-Irish descent, and settled many years before the Revolution in the Mecklenburg district, twelve miles northeast of Charlotte, at what is still known as the old Barry tanyard.

Though best known as a member of the Mecklenburg Convention of May, 1775, he performed many other services of a useful character, having served many years as a magistrate and a member of the County Court, and though advanced in life, he set the good example of taking his place among the

Mecklenburg troops when their services were called into requisition. At the age of 55 he fought as valiantly as the younger soldiers in disputing the passage of Cornwallis's army at Cowan's Ford, in February, 1781, when the lamented Davidson was slain, and aided in burying his body by torchlight in the graveyard at Hopewell. Mr. Barry was long a ruling elder in Hopewell Church. The first sermon by a Presbyterian clergyman in that section of the county was preached under the shade of a tree at the side of his house. His death occurred August 21, 1801, in the 75th year of his age.

JOHN FLENNIKIN

James and John Flennikin, descendants from Scotch-Irish ancestors, were among the early settlers of that race in Pennsylvania. They had nine children, of whom John Flennikin, the subject of this sketch, was the seventh, born in Pennsylvania, March 7, 1744. The family early migrated to Mecklenburg, and settled on the waters of McAlpin's Creek, in what is now Sharon Township. John Flennikin seems to have had a fair education, but beyond his service as a member of the Mecklenburg Convention of May, 1775, and many years as a magistrate and member of the County Court, we have no record. His life was one mainly of peaceful pursuits. He lived to a good old age, when he was thrown from his horse on his way to church and killed, and his remains mingle with the dust of Providence burial ground. His brother, David Flennikin, served under Colonel Irwin and General Sumter at the battle of Hanging Rock, where he was wounded, and carried to the hospital at Charlotte. He long enjoyed a pension for the wounds he received in the service, and died April 26th, 1826, in the 78th year of his age, and was buried in Providence graveyard. Both of the brothers left numerous and worthy descendants.

WILLIAM GRAHAM

But little can be gathered of this delegate to the Mecklenburg Convention of May, 1775. His was a farmer's life, quietly spent in his calling, and he left behind him few evidences of his public career. He was an Irishman and early settled in Mecklenburg County. He was useful in his day, serving, it is believed, in the army. He died at an advanced age in 1820 or 1822, near Davidson College.

MATTHEW M'CLURE

In the north of Ireland and about 1725, was Matthew McClure born, where he married; then came to America and settled in Mecklenburg about 1751, five miles south of Davidson College. It is an evidence of his worth that he was chosen one of the delegates to the Mecklenburg Convention of May, 1775. It is not known that he filled any other public position. His home was a rendezvous for the patriots of his section. In January, 1782, the County Court ordered that no person in Charlotte, or within two miles of the place, should be permitted to sell any spiritous liquors, so long as the hospital was continued in that town, and employed Matthew McClure to take possession of all such contraband liquors for the use of the hospital, or as the commanding officer should direct. Too old himself to enter active service in the field, his sons were much engaged in the army.

JOHN QUEARY

A native of Scotland, John Queary first migrated to Pennsylvania, and then to Mecklenburg some years before the Revolution. As early as January, 1770, we find Mr. Queary residing in what was called for a time Clear Creek, now Philadelphia, in the bounds of Rocky River, and was an elder in that church.

Of his Revolutionary service, save that he was a member of the Mecklenburg Convention of May, 1775, nothing is known. He is represented as a man of strong and vigorous intellect, and a good scholar, especially in mathematics; accumulating means to a moderate extent; died at an early period. He is buried in what was once Mecklenburg, now Union County.

EZRA ALEXANDER

All that can be stated of Mr. Alexander in addition to his having been a delegate to the Mecklenburg Convention of May, 1775, is that he headed a company in June and July, 1780, in Col. W. L. Davidson's command, during the Tory rising at Ramsour's Mill, and in the affair near Calson's Mill with a body of Tories while in pursuit of Bryan's party, and the next month served in Capt. John Brownfield's company of —— Regiment at the battle of Hanging Rock. (MS. Letters of Dr. C. L. Hunter, September 21, 1775.) He died in the summer of 1800, at an advanced age.

WAIGHTSTILL AVERY

The Avery family trace a Hungarian origin. Capt. James Avery, of Devonshire, England, came over with Winthrop's company in 1630, only ten years after the *Mayflower,* first settling at Gloucester; then in 1651 at New London, Conn., and shortly after at Groton. From him descended Waightstill Avery, the subject of this sketch, who was born in Groton May 3, 1743. He graduated at Princeton College in 1766, where he remained a tutor for a year. Then removing to Maryland, he studied law for about a year and a half under the direction of Littleton Dennis, where early in 1769 he set out for North Carolina.

Selecting Mecklenburg for his home, he domiciled with Hezekiah Alexander at the moderate rate of £12 (twelve pounds) per eight months.

In 1771 he was made prisoner by the Regulators at Yadkin Ferry, and carried to their camp in the woods. They gave him a flogging and soon set him at liberty. When the great war came he was prepared to meet it. In such an atmosphere as Mecklenburg, he could only learn to breathe the purest sentiments of patriotism. In the Mecklenburg Convention in May, 1775, he filled an honored place. He was most probably associated with Brevard and Kennon on the committee that reported the memorable Resolves of May 20th, and could scarcely have kept silent in enforcing their adoption by his talents and persuasive powers of eloquence. He was a "shrewd lawyer," said Prof. F. M. Hubbard, "whose integrity, no less than his deliberate wisdom, made his counsels weighty."

Jones, in his "Revolutionary Defense of North Carolina," states that Brevard and Avery, with their classical attainments, with the native talent and enthusiasm of Thomas Polk, produced the Mecklenburg Declaration. He was returned one of the Mecklenburg representatives to the North Carolina Provincial Congress of August and September, 1775, when he was chosen one of the two members for the Salisbury District of Provincial Council of Safety. The Council held two sessions that year, one in October and one in December.

He was dispatched, in behalf of the Council, to purchase from the South Carolina Committee of Safety 2,000 pounds of powder for the use of the Province, and was also appointed one of the committee for the District of Salisbury to purchase materials and to employ proper persons to make and repair guns and bayonets, and purchase guns, lead, and flints. In April, 1776, he was appointed chairman of four commissioners by the Provincial Congress to erect salt works and manufacture salt for the use of the public, which proved successful and of great importance.

He was in this year, 1777, appointed one of the trustees of Liberty Hall Academy at Charlotte, and was also chosen one of the two members to represent Mecklenburg in the House of Commons, and served on the committee to revise the whole body of the public laws of the State. On the 12th of January, 1778, he was commissioned Attorney-General of the State.

To the last his was the costume of the Revolution—short breeches, long waistcoats, silk stockings, and knee buckles—wearing his hair in a cue, and presenting altogether a singular appearance to the younger generation. Absent-mindedness was one of his peculiarities, of which his more intimate friends would take occasion to play off practical jokes at his expense. He was devoted to his friends and strong in his prejudices. He was very fond of his books and newspapers. He died in March, 1821.

COL. WILLIAM KENNON

The Kennons migrated from England and settled in Virginia about as early as 1660. Richard Kennon, with three associates, obtained a grant from the Colony of 2,827 acres in Henrico County, April 1, 1670, and Elizabeth Kennon, perhaps the widow of Richard, April 24, 1703, secured a grant of 4,000 acres in Henrico. Robert, William, and Richard Kennon, Jr., were the sons of this early couple.

William Kennon, recorded as "Gentleman," between April 17, 1725, and November, 1750, obtained five grants of land in Henrico, aggregating 4,063, and one tract of 4,000 acres in Prince George County. (MS. Letters of R. A. Brock, Corresponding Secretary Virginia Historical Society, September 13, 1875.)
He was probably there on professional business, and was invited as a matter of courtesy to a seat in the Convention in Charlotte May 20, 1775.

COL. JAMES HARRIS

According to the late Hon. W. S. Harris, an intelligent chronicler of the family, the Harris connection of Mecklenburg and Cabarrus were of Scotch-Irish stock, natives of Harrisburg, Penn., who emigrated first to Cecil County, Maryland, and in 1740 to North Carolina. The facts are that James Harris, a native of Yorkshire, England, first settled on the Susquehanna in 1719. But Harrisburg was not laid out as a town till sixty-five years after. A grandson of the first settler bore the name of Robert, a family name among the North Carolina Harrises. An immediate descendant of Col. James Harris states that he was a native of Wales, born April 3, 1739, but the probabilities are that he was of Welsh descent, and a native of Pennsylvania. He early settled on Clear Creek, in Mecklenburg County. He proved himself a leader among the people, and was chosen a delegate to the Mecklenburg Convention of May, 1775. In June, 1780, we find him serving as major of Colonel Irwin's regiment, and marching against the Tories at Ramsour's, who were defeated a little before the arrival of the rear unde. General Rutherford and Colonel Irwin. He was subsequently promoted to be colonel.

In 1785 he was chosen to represent Mecklenburg in the State Senate, a high honor in a region where there were so many able and worthy men. His death occurred September 27, 1797, in the 59th year of his age. He is represented as a very rich man, quiet in his demeanor, provident and successful, and a member of the Presbyterian denomination. Some of his descendants reside in Texas. His younger brother, Samuel Harris, a soldier of the Revolution, lived till he was 80 years old. Another brother, Robert Harris, will receive a special notice.

DAVID REESE

David Reese, a native of Wales, was among the Protestant emigrants who were induced to settle in Ireland. He was a Presbyterian preacher, and took part in the terrible siege of Londonderry, which lasted eight months, on scanty allowance. He subsequently returned to Wales, where his son, David Reese, was born in 1710, and came to America when a lad about 15 years old. He settled in Pennsylvania, where in due time he married Susan Polk, a near relative of Thomas and Ezekiel Polk, where their son Thomas was born in 1742, who subsequently became a distinguished clergyman in the Presbyterian Church. About 1750 David Reese emigrated, with his young family, and located in Poplar Tent settlement of the Catawba country.

Well educated for his day, he became a prominent man among the early settlers, and was chosen one of a bench of Poplar Tent Church elders in 1751. Waightstill Avery, in Diary of September, 1767, records: "Went to David Reese's, plotted a piece of land for him," and "wrote a deed for him to his son"; which would indicate wealth in the rich land of the country. He is one of the reputed delegates to the Mecklenburg Convention of May, 1775; was long a magistrate and member of the County Court.

Though too old to take the field, he was appointed by the Provincial Congress of April, 1776, with Thomas, to procure, purchase, and receive firearms for the use of the troops of Mecklenburg. He lived to see his country free and happy. His will bears date of February 5, 1787, and was admitted to probate in September following. He must have died not long before the latter date, at the age of about 77 years. His remains lie buried in Poplar Tent burial ground, in an unknown grave.

"He was a born statesman," writes Hon. W. S. Harris, and "one of the best of men." He was commanding in appearance, fine looking, with bright black eyes.

HENRY DOWNS

Of Scotch-Irish descent, Henry Downs was born in 1728, probably in Pennsylvania, and early settled in Providence settlement, which subsequently became a part of Mecklenburg.

Of his public career we only know that he was one of the reputed delegates to the famous Mecklenburg Convention. He lived to see his country free, and to enjoy the blessings of a well-spent life. He died October 8, 1798, at the age of 70 years, and was buried in Providence burial ground, 12 miles south of Charlotte. One correspondent speaks of "Henry Downs of precious memory," indicative of his worthy character, and the good name he left behind him. His sons, Thomas and Samuel Downs, were well known in their day, and their descendants are quite numerous in the Mecklenburg region.

JOHN FOARD

There was a John Foard in Somerset County, on the eastern shore of Maryland, a Presbyterian elder, as early as 1710, mentioned in the first stories of Foote's Sketches of Virginia. As that region furnished many of the early settlers of Mecklenburg, it is most probable that the John Foard of Mecklenburg was descended from that Maryland Presbyterian family of the same name.

As early as January 27, 1770, he is found among the members of Clear Creek congregation. He is said to have been one of the delegates to the Mecklenburg Convention of May, 1775, and long served as a magistrate and member of the County Court. He served as a private in Col. Charles Polk's Dragoons in the fall of 1781, on the Raft Swamp expedition. His will bears date of April 25, 1798, and he probably died not long after this period.

Mr. Harris represents him as a worthy and good man, possessing great courage. He lived and died in that part of Mecklenburg which now forms Union County. There are none of his lineal descendants remaining in the old Mecklenburg region, but a good many kindred bear his name.

CHARLES ALEXANDER

Of this member of the numerous Alexander family, little is known save that he was one of the reputed delegates to the Mecklenburg Convention of May, 1775. He lived on the line from Waxhaw to Charlotte. He was a gallant and true patriot, and unlike most of his Alexander kindred, he was an unbeliever in the Christian religion. His death took place in 1801. He had a grandson recently deceased, who was an officer and soldier in the war with Mexico.

ROBERT HARRIS, SR.

In the notice of Col. James Harris, a brother of the subject of this sketch, it was stated that he was descended from Welsh ancestry, and was probably a native of Pennsylvania.

Robert Harris, born about 1741, is also supposed to have been born in that State, and certain it is that the family connection included probably the parents and their sons, James, Robert, Samuel, Charles, and Thomas, and an only sister, who became the wife of Rev. Thomas Reese, early migrated to the Catawba Valley. Hon. W. S. Harris, who descended from

Charles, fixed the period of their migration in 1740; but it was probably a few years later, else some of the brothers and the sister must have been born in Mecklenburg County. The venerable Rev. N. R. Morgan and lady, the latter a granddaughter of Robert Harris, thinks he came to North Carolina with the early crowd of emigrants from Pennsylvania or Maryland.

As early as May, 1771, he was chosen an elder of Poplar Tent Church. (The Robert Harris of this sketch should not be confounded with the Col. Robert Harris, of Reed Creek, referred to in Foote's "Sketches of North Carolina," page 480.) Rev. Humphrey Hunter included the name of Richard Harris, Sr., among the list of delegates to the Mecklenburg Convention, which the Legislative Committee in the State pamphlet of 1831 adopted in the second organized list of *bona fide* members.

Lossing, in his "Field Book of the Revolution," corrects the apparent error of Richard Harris and substitutes the name of Robert Harris. "It is surprising," writes W. S. Harris, who lived all his life in that region, and one of the best chroniclers in that section of country, "that such an error should have been committed, and the name given as Richard; it is a mistake. I know that the name should have been Robert Harris."

It is due to truth to say that Rev. N. R. Morgan and lady, the latter his granddaughter, who remembered him personally, state that they never understood that that Robert Harris was one of the famous Mecklenburg delegates.

In view of his services and sufferings, a grant of 5,000 acres of land was donated to him in Tennessee, which was neglected for many years, but finally secured by his descendants, proving of great value to them. He became the possessor of a large body of land around what is now known as Harris's Station, on the North Carolina Railroad, in Cabarrus County. The mill he built on Rocky River, the dam of which is solid rock, still stands and continues to be known as Harris's Mill.

MAJ. JOHN DAVIDSON

Robert Davidson and wife, Mary Ramsay, of Dundee, Scotland, became early settlers of Chestnut Level, Lancaster County, Pennsylvania, where their son, John Davidson, was born December 15, 1735. With respectable education, and reared to the occupation of a farmer, and while yet a young man, about 1760, he migrated to the Catawba country, in North Carolina.

Here he was united in marriage with Violet, daughter of Samuel Wilson, and sister to the wife of Ezekiel Polk, and settled on the Catawba near Tool's Ford. Such was his prominence that he was chosen, in conjunction with Capt. Thomas Polk, to represent Mecklenburg County in the Colonial Legislature in 1773. When such a man as John Davidson states positively that he was one of the members of the famous Mecklenburg Convention of May, 1775, chosen in his captain's company, with John McKnitt Alexander as his coadjutor, no one has ever called this claim into question. It should stand as one of the fixed facts of history. How Dr. M. Winslow Alexander, in making up his list of delegates in 1824, should have omitted him, then being a venerable survivor of the Revolution and sustaining the highest character, with Gen. Joseph Graham among his honored sons-in-law, and how the Legislative Committee of 1831 should have ignored his claim to that undoubted honor and placed other names of doubtful import in their recognized list of delegates, is not the least of many strange things connected with this Mecklenburg matter. An intelligent gentleman states that his grandfather, Major Davidson, rode home the night after the declaration was made, fourteen miles, taking by-paths for fear of being killed by the enemy, when in truth there were no British soldiers within hundreds of miles of Mecklenburg in May, 1775; no Tories, of whom there were few in that region at any time, had shown themselves in hostile array. The Indians were still peaceful on the frontiers and remained so for more than a year later, and no Redcoats trod the soil of Mecklenburg till after Cornwallis forced himself there in September, 1780.

In September, 1775, he was appointed second major of Colonel Polk's regiment, and doubtless went with the regiment on the Snow Campaign at the close of the year against the Tory insurgents in the region of Ninety-Six, South Carolina. He was promoted to first major of Mecklenburg militia under Col. Adam Alexander and Lieutenant Phifer in April, 1776, and in the spring of that year, then in the summer and fall of the same year, he went on Rutherford's campaign against the Cherokees. No particulars are mentioned of his other services. The remainder of his long life he continued to reside at his old homestead on the Catawba until the death of his wife and marriage of his children, when, in 1824, he went to reside with his daughter, Mrs. W. Lee Davidson, near Davidson College, where he closed his long and useful life January 10, 1832, in the 97th year of his age, and was buried in the family burying ground at his former home, a spot selected by himself, near Tool's Ford, on the Catawba.

COL. EZEKIEL POLK

Captain Jack included in his list of those "who appeared to take the lead" in the Mecklenburg movement of May, 1775, Col. Ezekiel Polk, Samuel Martin, William Wilson, and Duncan Ochiltree; and Lossing has given the names of the three latter in his enumeration of the delegates. They were all doubtless prominent actors among the people on the interesting occasion. Of William Polk's eight children, a sketch of Col. Thomas Polk, the eldest, has already been given. Ezekiel was the youngest, born in Pennsylvania, December 7, 1747. "Pennsylvania born, and Carolina bred," as he himself composed in evidence for his tombstone, would imply that when quite young he followed the fortunes of his brothers to Carolina, and was mostly raised, or bred, as he preferred to term it. Of his youthful days, nothing is remembered.

He early married Mary Wilson, a sister to the wife of Maj. John Davidson. In 1769 he was clerk of the Court of Tryon County—territory from which Lincoln and Rutherford have since been formed.

In 1778, Colonel Polk removed into Mecklenburg County, eleven miles south of Charlotte, where his son, James K. Polk,* was born. This was a period of quiet in this region, and remained so until Cornwallis's invasion in September, 1780. There was no regular army then, after Gates's defeat, to protect the county. When Cornwallis reached Colonel Polk's, on Sugar Creek, in order to save the burning of his home, the destruction of his property, and the suffering of his family, he was forced to take British protection, which merely was understood to protect himself, family and property from molestation, without implying any pledge for sympathy or service.

CAPT. JAMES JACK

The bearer of the Mecklenburg Resolves of May, 1775, to Philadelphia—Capt. James Jack—was of Irish descent, born in Pennsylvania in 1739, whence he removed to North Carolina, and settled in Charlotte eight or ten years before the commencement of the Revolutionary War. He married Margaret Houston, and was long a popular hotel keeper in Charlotte. He took a decided and active part in the Revolutionary War. He probably served under Col. Thomas Polk on the Snow Campaign in 1775.

---

*James K. Polk was the son of Samuel Polk, and grandson of Ezekiel Polk.—EDITOR.

His large acquaintance with the people enabled him to raise a company of men, whom he led forth on Rutherford's Cherokee campaign in 1776. He was with the troops embodied who opposed Cornwallis when he entered Charlotte in September, 1781. Captain Jack also led his company in General Polk's brigade in April, 1781, joining General Greene at Rugeby's Mills, and serving a three months' tour of duty. The particulars of other services of Captain Jack are not preserved. It is only known that he was ever ready for service, and was so popular with his company that they induced him not to seek or accept the promotions, which indeed he did not desire. In a certificate extracted by Colonel Abraham and Hezekiah Alexander, December 24, 1781, it is stated that Captain Jack had resided several years in Mecklenburg County, was a good and worthy member of society, both civil and religious, and since the beginning of the war had always conducted himself as a patriot and as an officer in such a manner as to evince his honest zeal and attachment to the cause of his country. The close of the war left him poor. He had freely advanced all he possessed in the great struggle, a portion of it as a loan to North Carolina. His unrequited claims at the time of his death upon North Carolina amounted to £7,446 State currency. In 1783, Captain Jack removed to Georgia, settling in Wilkes County.

REV. FRANCIS CUMMINGS, D. D.

A child of Irish parentage, Mr. Cummings was born near Shippenburg, Penna., in the spring of 1752. In his 19th year his parents moved to Mecklenburg County, and young Cummings exchanged his former life for the classic halls of the Queen's Museum in Charlotte, where he was an eye-witness of the Mecklenburg Convention of May, 1775, concerning which he furnished a certificate, and also gave some account in a published sermon. He graduated at Queen's Museum about 1776, and spent several years teaching. Among his pupils in Bethel, York County, South Carolina, was Andrew Jackson, afterwards President, and William Smith, a United States Senator from South Carolina.

When licensed to preach he occupied various pulpits at Hopewell, Bethel, and other places. In 1788, while residing at Bethel, he was chosen by the people of York County a member of the South Carolina Convention for deciding upon the Constitution of the United States. Mr. Cummings was at various periods the pastor of some twenty congregations, some in North Carolina, South Carolina, and Georgia, dividing his time between teaching and preaching.

His last sermon was preached January 15, 1832, and three days later he was seized with influenza, which terminated his life at Greensboro, Ga., on the 2d of the ensuing February, in the 80th year of his age. He left behind him a good name and many descendants.

GEN. JOSEPH GRAHAM

A native of Pennsylvania, Joseph Graham was born October 13, 1759. His widowed mother in 1766 removed with her five children to North Carolina, settling in the vicinity of Charlotte, where Joseph received the most of his education. He was present during the meeting of the famous Mecklenburg Convention, and his reminiscences concerning it are not only the most detailed of any preserved, but the most important in citing facts connected with the Resolves which, when those of May 20th were subsequently discovered, go to substantiate that they were the real and only Resolves adopted by the people of Mecklenburg in May, 1775.

In May, 1778, when 19 years old, he enlisted in the Fourth Regiment of the North Carolina line, and marched into Caswell County, and was subsequently furloughed home; but in August was ordered to South Carolina, and then to Georgia; was in the battle of Stono, June 20, 1779, and soon after discharged. The next year he was appointed adjutant of the Mecklenburg regiment, and when the British army, under Lord Cornwallis, invaded the country in September, 1780, he was ordered by General Davidson to take command of such of the inhabitants as should collect in Charlotte on the news of the enemy's approach, who amounted to fifty in number. When the British entered Charlotte, September 26th, Major Davis and Captain Graham made a daring resistance, brief, but unavailing. They were compelled to retreat, but resisted as they retired. In one of the enemy's charges, Graham received nine wounds, six from the sabre and three from bullets. His stock buckles probably prevented one of the cuts upon his neck from fatally wounding him. As it was, he ever afterwards bore marks of the severity of the blow aimed at his life. Four deep sabre gashes scarred his head and one his side. He was left for dead when the enemy departed, and with difficulty crawled to some water near by, where, slaking his intolerable thirst, he washed his numerous painful wounds as well as he could.

For a time he expected to die unnoticed in this secluded spot, but by night was discovered by kind-hearted people who were in search of their wounded countrymen, and conveyed to a neighboring house of a widow. Here he was concealed in an upper room and was attended by the widow and her daughter during the night, expecting he might soon die. Once he slept and breathed so quietly, and was so pale, they thought he was dead. The next day a British officer's wife, with a company of horsemen, visited the widow's house in quest of fresh provisions. By some means she discovered that there was a wounded person in the loft, and, pressing the inquiry, learned he was an officer and his wounds severe, and kindly offered to send a British surgeon to dress his wounds as soon as she should reach the camp at Charlotte. Alarmed at his discovery and dreading to fall into the hands of the enemy, he rallied all his powers and caused himself to be placed on horseback the ensuing night and taken to his mother's, and not long after to the hospital. Three balls were taken from his body.

GEN. GEORGE GRAHAM

Nearly two years the senior of his brother, Joseph, whose career has just been sketched, George Graham was also a native of Pennsylvania, born in 1758, and when some nine years of age was brought to Mecklenburg County by his widowed mother, and educated at the Queen's Museum Academy at Charlotte, and became strongly imbued with the republican principles of the Scotch-Irish of that region. He was one of the party of young patriots who rode from Charlotte to Salisbury early in June, 1775, and arrested Dunn and Boothe, a couple of prominent Tory lawyers who proposed to detain Captain Jack when on his way to Philadelphia with the Resolves of the Mecklenburg Convention. He was active in harassing and thwarting the foraging parties of the enemy when Cornwallis lay at Charlotte, and one of the gallant fourteen who dared to attack, October 3, 1780, and actually drove a British foraging party of 450 infantry, 60 cavalry, and about 40 wagons, under Major Doyle, at McIntire's, seven miles north of Charlotte.

Capt. James Thompson commanded this daring party of Mecklenburgers. Two hundred yards from McIntire's was a thicket down a spring branch, to which Thompson and his party repaired. A point of rocky ridge, covered with bushes, passed obliquely from the road toward the spring, and within fifty steps of the house, which sheltered them from view. From under this cover Thompson and party deployed into line ten or twelve feet apart, and advanced silently to their intended position. The British were much out of order; some in the barn throwing down oats for the horses, others racing after the pigs, ducks and chickens; a squad was robbing the bee hive, while others were pillaging the dwelling. A sentinel placed on watch, within a few steps of where the Americans were advancing, appeared to be alarmed, though he had not seen them. Captain Thompson fired the first shot and brought down the sentinel. This being the signal for the attack, each man, as he could get a view, took ready and deliberate aim before he fired at the distance of 60 to 70 steps. In two instances where two happened to aim at the same pillager, when the first fired and the fellow fell, the second had to change his aim and search for another object.

The enemy immediately began to form and fire briskly. None of the Americans had time to load and fire the second time, except Captain Thompson and Bradley, who were the first to discharge their rifles. The last shot of Thompson's was aimed at the captain of the party at the barn, 150 steps distant, who died of the wound he received two days afterwards, at the house of Samuel McCombs, in Charlotte. Thompson's party retreated through the thicket, which was nearly parallel to the great road, and only about one-half mile from it. The enemy continued to fire briskly and ceased about the time the Americans were half a mile away. The main body of the British under Major Doyle, who were in the rear, hearing the firing at McIntire's, became alarmed and hurried to the support of their friends. Captain Thompson's party now loaded their rifles, ascended the creek bottom, deployed, as before, under cover of a high bank parallel with the road, and about 40 rods from it. They had not been long at this station before the enemy's advance, and some wagons, came on. They severally fired, taking deliberate aim, and then retreated down the creek. When the front of the enemy's column arrived near the creek's ford, they formed and commenced a tremendous fire through the low ground, which continued till Thompson's army had retreated near a half mile. The cavalry at the same time divided, one-half passing down each side of the creek. Simultaneous with this movement, six or seven hounds came in full cry on the track of the retreating Americans, and in about three-quarters of a mile came up with them. One of the dogs was shot, and the others seemed to comprehend the situation and made no further noise. The country being thickly covered with undergrowth, Thompson's men escaped unhurt. The British cavalry kept on their flank on the high ground until they reached the plantation of Robert Carr, Sr., where they appeared much enraged, and carried the old gentleman, though 70 years old, a prisoner to Charlotte. Major Doyle's party moved on from the ford of the creek and formed a

Declaration of Independence

junction with those at McIntire's farm; gathered up eight dead and twelve wounded, put them in their wagons and retreated to Charlotte in great haste. On their arrival they reported that they had found a rebel in every bush after passing seven miles in that direction. The names of those fourteen deserve to be perpetuated in Mecklenburg history, namely: Capt. James Thompson, George Graham, Frank Bradley (killed a few days after by four of Bryan's Tories), James Henry, Thomas and John Dickson, John Long, Robert and John Robinson, George and Hugh Theston, Thomas McClure, and Edward and George Shipley. It is believed that during the whole war the enemy did not sustain so great a loss nor meet with so complete a disappointment in his objects by such a mere handful of men. That out of 30 shots fired, 20 should have done execution, is quite a new experience in the history of war, and several of Thompson's men thought that every shot would have told, so deliberate was their aim, had each singled out a different object; but in two or more instances, aiming at the same person. (Gen. Joseph Graham's narrative in *North Carolina University Magazine,* March, 1836.)

APPENDIX

Documents Cited in Preceding Address

Martin's Preface

* * * * * * * * * * * * *

"Imperfect as the present publication is, it began to engage the attention of the writer as early as the year 1791; at that period, the legislature of North Carolina afforded him some aid, in the publication of a collection of the statutes of the parliament of England, then in force and use within that state. In preparing that work, he examined all the statutes from Magna Charta to the Declaration of Independence, and an arrangement of all those which related to America, afforded him a complete view of the colonial system of England. In 1803 he was employed by the same legislature to publish a revisal of the acts of the general assembly, passed during the proprietary, royal and state governments, and the local information he acquired in carrying into effect the intentions of those who employed him, suggested the idea of collecting materials for a history of the state; and when afterwards he had the honor of representing the town of Newbern in the house of commons, he was favored with a resolution of the general assembly, authorizing the secretary of state to allow him access to the records of his office. In the speeches of the governors, at the opening of the sessions of the legislature, he found a reference to the principal transactions during recess, and there were few important events, particularly relating to the state, which left no trace on the journals of the legislature, or the proceedings of the executive.

"During several journeys, which he afterwards made to several parts of the country, he received considerable information from individuals. Mr. George Pollock of Newbern, confided to him an official letter book, and several documents left by one of his ancestors, who came to the county of Albemarle, in the latter part of the seventeenth century, and who, in the beginning of the following, exercised the functions of chief magistrate over the northern part of Carolina. The late governor Johnson, a nephew of Gabriel Johnson, who presided over the affairs of the province from the year 1734 to 1754; governor Smith, who was in possession of the papers of president Rowan, and governor Ashe, whose ancestors were among the earliest settlers of the country, afforded considerable materials. The gentlemen in possession of the records of the Quaker meetings, in Perquimans and Pasquotank counties, and the head of the *Unitas Fratrum,* or Moravian Brethren, cheerfully yielded their assistance.

"A citizen of North Carolina, being a citizen of the United States, has a right to expect, in a history of his own state, some notice, not only of the settlement of, but also of the most prominent events that took place in the sister states; and as the affairs of the mother country have necessarily a considerable influence on those of her colonies, the principal wars, in which England was engaged, must necessarily be noticed in the history of any of her American provinces. Under these impressions, the necessary information, in this respect, was sought in the most approved publications.

"The writer imagined, he had collected sufficient material to justify the hope of producing a history of North Carolina, worth the attention of his fellow citizens, and he had arranged all those that related to transactions, anterior to the declaration of independence, when, in 1809, Mr. Madison thought his services were wanted, first in the Mississippi territory and afterwards in that of Orleans; and when the latter territory became a state, the new government thought proper to retain him.

"He had entertained the hope, that the time would arrive when disengaged from public duties, he might resume the work he had commenced in Carolina; but years have rolled away, without bringing this period; and a shock his health lately received during the year of his great climacteric, has warned him, that the moment is arrived when his intended work must engage his immediate attention, or be absolutely abandoned.

"A circumstance, for some time, recommended the latter alternative. The public prints stated, that a gentleman of known industry and great talents, who has filled a very high office in North Carolina, was engaged in a similar work; but several years have elapsed since, and nothing favors the belief that the hopes which he excited, will soon be realized.

"This gentleman had made application for the materials now published, and they would have been forwarded to him, if they had been in a condition of being useful to any but him who had collected them. In their circuitous way from Newbern to New York and New Orleans, the sea water found its way to them: since their arrival, the mice, worms, and a variety of insects of humid and warm climate, have made great ravages among them. The ink of several very ancient documents has grown so pale, as to render them nearly illegible, and notes hastily taken on a journey, are in so cramped a hand, that they are not to be deciphered by any person but he who made them.

"The determination has been taken to put the work immediately to press in the condition it was when it reached New Orleans: this has prevented any use being made of Williamson's History of North Carolina, a copy of which did not reach the writer's hands till after his arrival in Louisiana.

"The expectation is cherished, that the people of North Carolina will receive, with indulgence a work, ushered to light under circumstances so untoward.

"Very ample notes and materials are ready for a volume, relating to the events of the revolutionary war, and another, detailing subsequent transactions, till the writer's departure from Newbern, in 1809.

If God yield him life and health, and his fellow citizens in North Carolina appear desirous these should follow the two volumes now presented to them, it is not improbable they will appear.

"Gentilly, near New Orleans,
"July 20, 1829."

PAMPHLET ISSUED BY THE LEGISLATURE OF NORTH CAROLINA, 1831

"THE DECLARATION OF INDEPENDENCE

"By the Citizens of Mecklenburg County, on the twentieth day of May, 1775, with accompanying documents, published by the Governor, under the authority and direction of the General Assembly of the State of North Carolina.

"PREFACE

"The resolution of the General Assembly directing this publication, makes it the duty of the Governor to cause to be published in pamphlet form the Report of the Committee relative to the Declaration of Independence, and the accompanying documents, in the following order, viz: 1. The Mecklenburg Declaration with the names of the Delegates composing the meeting. 2. The certificates testifying to the circumstances attending the Declaration; 3. The proceedings of the Cumberland Association.

"In the discharge of this duty, the Governor has deemed it proper to prefix to the publication the following brief review of the evidence by which the authenticity of this interesting portion of the history of North Carolina is controverted and sustained.

"On the 30th of April, 1819, the publication marked A made its appearance in the *Raleigh Register*. It was communicated to the editors of that paper by Dr. Joseph McKnitt, then and now a citizen of the county of Mecklenburg, and was speedily republished in most of the newspapers in the Union. A paper containing it (the *Essex Register*) was, it seems, on the 22d June, 1819, enclosed to Mr. Jefferson, by his illustrious compatriot, John Adams, accompanied with the remark, that he thought it genuine; and this suggestion of Mr. Adams elicited the following reply, which was at that time published in various newspapers, and has been since given to the world in the 4th volume of Mr. Jefferson's Works, page 314:

"TO JOHN ADAMS

"*'Monticello, July* 9, 1819.

"'DEAR SIR,—I am in debt to you for your letters of May the 21st, 27th, and June the 22nd. The first, delivered me by Mr. Greenwood, gave me the gratification of his acquaintance; and a gratification it always is, to be made acquainted with gentleman of candor, worth, and information, as I found Mr. Greenwood to be. That on the subject of Mr.

Samuel Adams Wells, shall not be forgotten in time and place, when it can be used to his advantage.

"'But what has attracted my peculiar notice, is the paper from Mecklenburg County, of North Carolina, published in the *Essex Register,* which you were so kind as to enclose in your last, of June the 22nd. And you seem to think it genuine. I believe it spurious. I deem it to be a very unjustifiable quiz, like that of the volcano, so minutely related to us as having broken out in North Carolina, some half dozen years ago, in that part of the country, and perhaps in that very county of Mecklenburg, for I do not remember its precise locality. If this paper be really taken from the *Raleigh Register,* as quoted, I wonder it should have escaped Ritchie, who culls what is good from every paper, as the bee from every flower; and the *National Intelligencer,* too, which is edited by a North Carolinian; and that the fire should blaze out all at once in Essex, one thousand miles from where the spark is said to have fallen. But if really taken from the *Raleigh Register,* who is the narrator, and is the name subscribed real, or is it as fictitious as the paper itself? It appeals, too, to an original book, which is burnt, to Mr. Alexander, who is dead, to a joint letter from Caswell, Hewes, and Hooper all dead, to a copy sent to the dead Caswell, and another sent to Doctor Williamson, now probably dead, whose memory did not recollect, in the history he has written of North Carolina, this gigantic step of its county of Mecklenburg. Horry, too, is silent in his history of Marion, whose scene of action was the country bordering on Mecklenburg. Ramsay, Marshall, Jones, Girardin, Wirt, historians of the adjacent States, all silent. When Mr. Henry's resolutions, far short of independence, flew like lightning through every paper, and kindled both sides of the Atlantic, this flaming declaration of the same date, of the independence of Mecklenburg County, of North Carolina, absolving it from the British allegiance, and abjuring all political connection with that nation, although sent to Congress, too, is never heard of. It is not known even a twelve-months after, when a similar proposition is first made in that body. Armed with this bold example, would not you have addressed our timid brethren in peals of thunder, on their tardy fears? Would not every advocate of independence have rung the glories of Mecklenburg County, in North Carolina, in the ears of the doubting Dickinson and others, who hung so heavily on us? Yet the example of independent Mecklenburg County, in North Carolina, was never once quoted. The paper speaks, too, of the continued exertions of their delegation (Caswell, Hooper, Hewes) "in the cause of liberty and independence." Now, you remember as well as I do, that we had not a greater Tory in Congress than Hooper; that Hewes was very wavering, sometimes firm, sometimes feeble, according as the day was clear or cloudy; that Caswell, indeed, was a good Whig, and kept these gentlemen to the notch, while he was present; but that he left us soon, and their line of conduct became then uncertain until Penn came, who fixed Hewes and the vote of the State.

I must not be understood as suggesting any doubtfulness in the State of North Carolina. No State was more fixed or forward. Nor do I affirm positively that this paper is a fabrication, because the proof of a negative can only be presumptive. But I shall believe it such until positive and solemn proof of its authenticity shall be produced. And if the name of McKnitt be real, and not a part of the fabrication, it needs a vindication by the production of such proof. For the present, I must be an unbeliever in the apocryphal gospel.

" 'I am glad to learn that Mr. Ticknor has safely returned to his friends; but should have been much more pleased had he accepted the Professorship in our University, which we should have offered him in form. Mr. Bowditch, too, refuses us; so fascinating is the *vinculum* of the *dulce natale solum*. Our wish is to procure natives, where they can be found, like these gentlemen, of the first order of acquirement in their respective lines; but preferring foreigners of the first order to the natives of the second, we shall certainly have to go, for several of our Professors, to countries more advanced in science than we are.

" 'I set out within three or four days for my other home, the distance of which, and its cross mails, are great impediments to epistolary communications. I shall remain there about two months; and there, here, and every where, I am, and shall always be, affectionately and respectfully yours,

" 'TH. JEFFERSON.'

"The republication of this letter in a work which is intended for, and will go down to posterity, recommended alike by its intrinsic excellence, and the illustrious name of the author, has imposed upon the Legislature the task of proving that, with regard to this particular fact, Mr. Jefferson was mistaken, and that his opinion was made up from a very superficial and inaccurate examination of the publication in the *Raleigh Register,* the only evidence then before him, and upon which his letter is a commentary.

"The letter itself was evidently written *currente calamo,* and for that reason may not be regarded as a fair subject for severe criticism. It is not intended to subject it to such a test, nor is it designed to examine it further than may be necessary to the ascertainment of truth. Of the ability, the purity, the patriotism of the author, it is unnecessary to speak. His love of country was not bounded by the confines of Virginia; but it is no discredit to his memory that her institutions, her heroes, and her statesmen occupied the first place in his affections. She was emphatically 'the mother of great men,' and 'his own, his native land'; and it is no matter of surprise that he should be unwilling, without the most ample proof, to transfer the brightest page of her history to emblazon the records of a sister State. Mr. Wirt's 'Life of Patrick Henry' had just been published, and for the latter was claimed the high distinction of having been the first to give motion to the ball of the Revolution. Mr. Jefferson

Declaration of Independence

himself was the author of the Declaration of Independence by Congress, and was not disposed to share in any degree the immortality with which it had crowned him, with a comparatively obscure citizen of North Carolina; and, therefore, the evidence which was at once satisfactory to Mr. Adams, is by him pronounced 'to be a very unjustifiable quiz.'

"The grounds for this opinion, in the order in which they are given to Mr. Adams, are, 1. That the story is 'like that of the volcano* having broken out in that part of the country, and perhaps in *that very county of Mecklenburg.*' 2. 'If this paper be *really* taken from the *Raleigh Register,* as quoted, I wonder it should have *escaped* Ritchie,' etc., 'and that the fire should blaze out all at once in Essex, one thousand miles from where the spark is said to have fallen.' 3. 'But if *really* taken from the *Raleigh Register, who is the narrator,* and is the *name* subscribed *real,* or is it as fictitious as the *paper itself?*' 4. 'It appeals, too, to an original book, which is *burnt,* to Mr. Alexander, who is *dead,* to a joint letter from Caswell, Hewes and Hooper, *all dead,* to a copy sent to the *dead Caswell,* and another sent to Dr. Williamson, *now probably dead,* whose memory did not recollect, in the history he has written of North Carolina, *this gigantic step of its county of Mecklenburg,*' etc., etc.

---

*"The hoax alluded to was published in 1812, and represented the volcano as having broken out in the neighborhood of the Warm Springs, in Buncombe, a point nearly as distant from the county of Mecklenburg as from Monticello.

"Without further remark with regard to the first point—*the quiz about the volcano*—or the second, whether the 'spurious' paper was *really* published in the *Raleigh Register*, it is proper to say, in reply to the *third argument,* that the *name subscribed is real,* that the individual still lives, that he is moreover a credible witness, and that it is to his laudable attention and exertions that the State is indebted for the preservation of much of the testimony which is now offered to the public. The *fourth argument* demands, and will receive more particular attention and examination.

"The paper appeals to a book, which is burnt; to Mr. Alexander, who is dead; to Messrs. Caswell, Hooper, and Hewes, all dead; to a copy sent to 'THE DEAD CASWELL,' and another sent to Dr. Williamson, probably dead, are the consecutive facts which *Mr. Jefferson* states, and on which he relies. Admit the premises, and the conclusion would be probable, though not inevitable; and a writer of much less ability, if permitted to *assume* his facts, might predicate upon them not only a very plausible, but an unanswerable argument. The very fact, however, on which Mr. Jefferson rests, as the climax of improbabilities, is not only not proved to exist, but, upon his own showing, does not exist; and justifies the remark in the outset, that his letter was written in haste, upon a very superficial and imperfect view of the subject. The paper does not appeal 'TO THE DEAD CASWELL,' but to the then LIVING DAVIE, a native of the section of country in which the event

DECLARATION OF INDEPENDENCE 159

occurred, like the former, a distinguished hero of the Revolution, and, in every respect, a proper depositary of the record. The following is the statement in question: (See the paper A.) ('The foregoing is a true copy of the papers, on the above subject, left in my hands by John McKnitt Alexander, dec'd. I find it mentioned on file that the original book was burned April, 1800. That a copy of the proceedings was sent to Hugh Williamson,* in New York, then writing a history of North Carolina, and that a copy was sent to Gen. W. R. Davie.') Gen. *Davie* died shortly after the date of Mr. Jefferson's letter; but this identical copy, known by the writer of these remarks to be in the hand-writing of John McKnitt Alexander, one of the secretaries of the Mecklenburg meeting, is now in the Executive Office of this State. (See Dr. Henderson's certificate, B.) *Caswell, Hooper,* and *Hewes* are all dead; but Capt. Jack, who was appointed to carry to them, at Philadelphia, this Mecklenburg Declaration, lived long enough to bear testimony to the truth; and his statement (C) is circumstantial, explicit, and satisfactory. If it needed confirmation, it would be

---

*"This copy the writer well recollects to have seen in the possession of Dr. Williamson, in the year 1793, in Fayetteville, together with a letter to him from John McKnitt Alexander, and to have conversed with him on the subject. Why it is not mentioned in his history, is not strange to any one who *knows the State,* and has *read* the book. It cannot be regarded as a *history* of any country. The memorable *Report and Resolutions* of the Congress of April, 1776, are alike unnoticed. A correct and satisfactory account of both proceedings will be found in the last chapter of Martin's History of North Carolina.

found to be fully sustained by the interesting communication (D) of the late Rev. Francis Cummins, D.D., of Georgia, to the Hon. Nathaniel Macon. More satisfactory evidence, drawn from more respectable sources, Mr. Jefferson, if alive, could not and would not require. It is not hazarding too much to say, that there is no one event of the Revolution which has been, or can be more fully or clearly authenticated.

"It is, perhaps, needless to multiply proofs, or to extend this article. Col. William Polk is a resident of this city, a venerable remnant of the Revolutionary stock, has passed the common boundary of human life, and in a green old age is in the full possession of his faculties. His compatriots, Caswell, and Hooper, and Hewes, *are dead, but he lives,* was present, heard his father proclaim the Declaration to the assembled multitude; and need it be inquired, in any portion of this Union, if *he* will be believed?

"The letter (E) of Gen. Joseph Graham, another surviving officer of the Revolution, a citizen and a soldier worthy of the best days of the Republic, will be read with pleasure and perfect confidence throughout the wide range of his acquaintance.

"The extract from the memoir of the late Rev. Humphrey Hunter (F), of Lincoln, is equally explicit, full, and satisfactory. He, with several other respectable gentlemen, whose statements are appended, was an eye-witness of what he relates; and the combined testimony of all these individuals prove the existence of the Mecklenburg Declaration, and all the circumstances connected with it, as fully and clearly as any fact can be shown by human testimony.

"The following extract from 'The Journal of the Provincial Congress of North Carolina, held at Halifax, on the 4th April, 1776' (pp. 11, 12), shows that the first *legislative recommendation* of a DECLARATION OF INDEPENDENCE by the CONTINENTAL CONGRESS, originated likewise in the State of North Carolina. It is worthy of remark, that *John McKnitt Alexander,* the Secretary of the meeting, *Waightstill Avery, John Phifer, and Robert Irwin,* who were conspicuous actors in the proceedings in Mecklenburg, were active and influential members of this Provincial Congress.

" 'The select committee to take into consideration the usurpations and violences attempted and committed by the King and Parliament of Britain against America, and the further measures to be taken for frustrating the same, and for the better defense of this Province, reported as follows, to wit:

" 'It appears to your committee, that pursuant to the plan concerted by the British Ministry for subjugating America, the King and Parliament of Great Britain have usurped a power over the persons and properties of the people unlimited and uncontrolled; and disregarding their humble petitions of peace, liberty, and safety, have made divers legislative acts, denouncing war, famine, and every species of calamity, against the Continent in general. The British fleets and armies have been, and still are daily employed in destroying the people, and committing the most horrid devastations on the country. That Governors in different Colonies have declared protection to slaves who should imbrue their hands in the blood of their masters. That the ships belonging to America are declared prizes of war, and many of them have been violently seized and confiscated. In consequence of all which multitudes of the people have been destroyed, or from easy circumstances reduced to the most lamentable distress.

"'And whereas the moderation hitherto manifested by the United Colonies, and their sincere desire to be reconciled to the mother country on constitutional principles, have procured no mitigation of the aforesaid wrongs and usurpations, and no hopes remain of obtaining redress by those means alone which have been hitherto tried, your committee are of opinion that the House should enter into the following resolve, to wit:

"'*Resolved*, That the DELEGATES FOR THIS COLONY IN THE CONTINENTAL CONGRESS BE IM POWERED TO CONCUR WITH THE DELEGATES OF THE OTHER COLONIES IN DECLARING INDEPENDENCY AND FORMING FOREIGN ALLIANCES, reserving to this Colony the sole and exclusive right of forming a Constitution and laws for this Colony, and o appointing Delegates from time to time (under the direction of a general representation thereof), to meet the Delegates of the other Colonies, for such purposes as shall be hereafter pointed out.

Declaration of Independence   163

" 'The Congress taking the same into consideration, *unanimously* concurred therewith.'

"The striking similarity of expression in the concluding sentences of the Mecklenburg Declaration, and the Declaration by Congress on the 4th of July, 1776, has been repeatedly urged and relied upon as disproving the authenticity of the former. It is scarcely necessary to reply to this suggestion. It is not very strange that men who think alike should speak alike upon the same subject, more especially when high-toned patriotic feeling seeks for utterance. This similarity of expression is not confined however, to these two papers. A comparison of the foregoing resolutions with the Declaration, as drawn by Mr. Jefferson, will satisfy the most credulous upon this subject. Who suspects Mr. Jefferson of intentional plagiarism? and yet he might be charged with having appropriated the language of the Provincial Legislature, with at least as much propriety as Mr. Alexander with having *forged* the Mecklenburg Declaration. The sentiments embodied by Mr. Jefferson were not peculiar to himself, but adopted by him as expressive of the common feeling in the common language of that eventful period.

"REPORT AND RESOLUTIONS

"Adopted by the General Assembly at the Session of 1830-31, *upon which this publication is predicated.*

"The committee to whom it was referred to examine, collate, and arrange in proper order such parts of the Journals of the Provincial Assemblies of North Carolina, as relate to the Declaration of American Independence; also such documents as relate to the Declaration of Independence made by the patriotic men of Mecklenburg in May, 1775; and also such measures as relate to the same cause, adopted by the freemen of Cumberland County, previous to the 4th of July, 1776, in order to the publication and distribution of such documents, having performed the duty assigned them, respectfully report:

"That upon an attentive examination of the Journals of the Provincial Assembly of North Carolina, which met at Halifax in the month of April 1776, the committee are of opinion, that no selection could be made from the said Journal to answer the purpose of the House. But as everything relating to that period must be interesting to those who value the blessing of national independence, the committee recommend that the whole of the Journal be printed, and receive the same extended distribution which the resolution of the House contemplates for the proceedings in Mecklenburg and Cumberland. This course is deemed by the committee the more proper, because the Journal is now out of print, and it is highly probable that the copy in the possession of the committee is the only one now extant.

"Your committee have also examined, collated, and arranged all the documents which have been accessible to them, touching the Declaration of Independence by the citizens of Mecklenburg, and the proceedings of the freemen of Cumberland.

Declaration of Independence 165

"By the publication of these papers it will be fully verified, that as early as the month of May, 1775, a portion of the people of North Carolina, sensible that their wrongs could no longer be borne, without sacrificing both safety and honor, and that redress so often sought, so patiently waited for, and so cruelly delayed, was no longer to be expected, did, by a public and solemn act, declare the dissolution of the ties which bound them to the crown and people of Great Britain, and did establish an independent, though temporary, government for their own control and direction.

"The first claim of Independence evinces such high sentiments of valor and patriotism, that we cannot, and ought not, lightly to esteem the honor of having made it. The fact of the Declaration should be announced, its language should be published and perpetuated, and the names of the gallant representatives of Mecklenburg, with whom it originated, should be preserved from an oblivion, which, should it involve them, would as much dishonor us, as injure them. If the thought of Independence did not first occur to them, to them, at least, belongs the proud distinction of having first given language to the thought; and it should be known, and, fortunately, it can still be conclusively established, that the Revolution received its first impulse toward Independence, however feeble, that impulse might have been, in North Carolina. The committee are aware that this assertion has elsewhere been received with doubt, and at times met with denial; and it is therefore believed to be more strongly incumbent upon the House to usher to the world the Mecklenburg Declaration, accompanied with such testimonials of its genuineness, as shall silence incredulity, and with such care for its general diffusion, as shall forever secure it from being forgotten. And in recounting the causes, the origin and the progress of our Revolutionary struggle, til its final issue in acknowledged independence, whatever the brilliant achievement of other States may have been, let it never be forgotten, that at a period of darkness and oppression, without concert with others, without assurances of support from any quarter, a few gallant North Carolinians, all fear o consequences lost in a sense of their country' wrongs, relying, under Heaven, solely upon them selves, nobly dared to assert, and resolved to maintain, that independence of which, whoever might have thought, none had then spoken; and thu earned for themselves, and for their fellow-citizen of North Carolina, the honor of giving birth to th first Declaration of Independence.

"The committee respectfully recommend the adoption of the following resolutions.

"All of which is submitted.

"Thos. G. Polk, Chairman
John Bragg,
Evan Alexander,
Louis D. Henry,
Alex. McNeill.

"*Resolved,* That his Excellency the Governor b directed to cause to be published in pamphlet form

Declaration of Independence

the above Report and the accompanying documents, in the manner and order following, viz.: After the Report, first, the Mecklenburg Declaration, with the names of the Delegates composing the meeting; second, the Certificates testifying to the circumstances attending the Declaration; third, the proceedings of the Cumberland Association. And that he be further directed to have reprinted, in like manner, separate and distinct from the above, the accompanying Journal of the Provincial Assembly, held at Halifax in 1776.

"*Resolved further,* That after publication, the Governor be instructed to distribute said documents as follows, to wit: Twenty copies of each to the Library of the State; to each of the Libraries at the University, ten copies; to the Library of the Congress of the United States, ten copies; and one copy to each of the Executives of the several States of the Union.

" 'DECLARATION OF INDEPENDENCE.

" 'May 20, 1775.

" '*Names of the Delegates Present.*

" 'COL. THOMAS POLK,   JNO. MCKNITT ALEXAN-
   EPHRAIM BREVARD,   DER.
   HEZEKIAH J. BALCH,   HEZEKIAH ALEXANDER,
   JOHN PHIFER,   ADAM ALEXANDER,
   JAMES HARRIS,   CHARLES ALEXANDER,
   WILLIAM KENNON,   ZACHEUS WILSON, Sen.

JOHN FORD, WAIGHTSTILL AVERY,
RICHARD BARRY, BENJAMIN PATTON,
HENRY DOWNS, MATTHEW MCCLURE,
EZRA ALEXANDER, NEIL MORRISON,
WILLIAM GRAHAM, ROBERT IRWIN,
JOHN QUEARY, JOHN FLENNIKEN,
ABRAHAM ALEXANDER, DAVID REESE,
JOHN DAVIDSON, RICHARD HARRIS, Sen.

" 'ABRAHAM ALEXANDER was appointed Chairman, and JOHN MCKNITT ALEXANDER, Clerk. The following resolutions were offered, viz.:

" '1st. *Resolved,* That whosoever directly or indirectly abetted, or in any way, form, or manner, countenanced the unchartered and dangerous invasion of our rights, as claimed by Great Britain, is an enemy to this country, to America, and to the inherent and inalienable rights of man.

" '2d. *Resolved,* That we, the citizens of Mecklenburg County, do hereby dissolve the political bands which have connected us to the mother country, and hereby absolve ourselves from all allegiance to the British Crown, and abjure all political connection, contract, or association, with that nation, who have wantonly trampled on our rights and liberties, and inhumanly shed the blood of American patriots at Lexington.

" '3d. *Resolved,* That we do hereby declare ourselves a free and independent people; are, and of righ* ought to be, a sovereign and self-governing Association, under the control of no power other than tha*

Declaration of Independence 169

of our God and the general government of the Congress; to the maintenance of which independence, we solemnly pledge to each other our mutual co-operation, our lives, our fortunes, and our most sacred honor.

" '4th. *Resolved,* That as we now acknowledge the existence and control of no law or legal officer, civil or military, within this county, we do hereby ordain and adopt as a rule of life, all, each and every of our former laws,—wherein, nevertheless, the Crown of Great Britain never can be considered as holding rights, privileges, immunities, or authority therein.

" '5th. *Resolved,* That it is further decreed, that all, each and every military officer in this county, is hereby reinstated in his former command and authority, he acting conformably to these regulations. And that every member present, of this delegation, shall henceforth be a civil officer, viz., a Justice of the Peace, in the character of a *"Committee-man,"* to issue process, hear and determine all matters of controversy, according to said adopted laws, and to preserve peace, union and harmony in said county;—and to use every exertion to spread the love of country and fire of freedom throughout America, until a more general and organized government be established in this province.

" 'After discussing the foregoing resolves, and arranging bye-laws and regulations for the government of a Standing Committee of Public Safety, who were selected from these delegates, the whole proceedings were unanimously adopted and signed. A select committee was then appointed to draw a more full and definite statement of grievances, and a more formal Declaration of Independence. The Delegation then adjourned about 2 o'clock A. M., May 20.'

"A.

"FROM THE RALEIGH REGISTER OF APRIL 30, 1819.

" 'IT is not probably known to many of our readers, that the citizens of Mecklenburg County, in this State, made a Declaration of Independence more than a year before Congress made theirs. The following document on the subject has lately come to the hands of the Editor from unquestionable authority and is published that it may go down to posterity.

" 'NORTH CAROLINA, MECKLENBURG COUNTY,

May 20, 1775.

" 'In the spring of 1775, the leading characters of Mecklenburg County, stimulated by that enthusiastic patriotism which elevates the mind above considerations of individual aggrandizement, and scorning to shelter themselves from the impending storm by submission to lawless power, etc., etc., held several detached meetings, in each of which the individual sentiments were, "that the cause of Boston was the cause of all; that their destinies were indissolubly connected with those of their Eastern fellow-citizens—and that they must either submit to all the impositions which an unprincipled, and to them unrepresented, Parliament might impose—or support their brethren who were doomed to sustain the first shock of that power, which, if successful there, would ultimately overwhelm all in the common calamity." Conformably to these principles, Colonel T. Polk, through solicitation, issued an order to each Captain's company in the county of Mecklenburg, (then comprising the present county of Cabarrus,) directing each militia company to elect two persons, and delegate to them ample power to devise ways and means to aid and assist their suffering brethren in Boston, and also generally to adopt measures to extricate themselves from the impending storm, and to secure unimpaired their inalienable rights, privileges and liberties, from the dominant grasp of British imposition and tyranny.

" 'In conformity to said order, on the 19th of May, 1775, the said delegation met in Charlotte, vested with unlimited powers; at which time official news, by express, arrived of the battle of Lexington on that day of the preceding month. Every delegate felt the value and importance of the prize, and the awful and solemn crisis which had arrived—every bosom swelled with indignation at the malice, inveteracy, and insatiable revenge, developed in the late attack at Lexington. The universal sentiment was: let us not flatter ourselves that popular harangues, or resolves; that popular vapor will avert the storm, or vanquish our common enemy—let us deliberate—let us calculate the issue—the probable result; and then let us act with energy, as brethren leagued to preserve our property—our lives—and what is still more endearing, the liberties of America. *Abraham Alexander* was then elected Chairman, and *John McKnitt Alexander,* Clerk. After a free and full discussion of the various objects for which the delegation had been convened, it was unanimously ordained—

[DAVIE COPY.]

" ' "1. *Resolved,* That whoever directly or indirectly abetted, or in any way, form, or manner, countenanced the unchartered and dangerous invasion of our rights, as claimed by Great Britain, is an enemy to this country—to America—and to the inherent and inalienable rights of man.

" ' "2. *Resolved,* That we, the citizens of Mecklenburg County, do hereby dissolve the political bands which have connected us with the Mother Country, and hereby absolve ourselves from all allegiance to the British Crown, and abjure all political connection, contract, or association with that nation, who have wantonly trampled on our rights and liberties—and inhumanly shed the innocent blood of American patriots at Lexington.

" ' "3. *Resolved,* That we do hereby declare ourselves a free and independent people, are, and of right ought to be, a sovereign and self-governing Association, under the control of no power other than that of our God and the General Government of the Congress; to the maintenance of which independence, we solemnly pledge to each other, our mutual co-operation, our lives, our fortunes, and our most sacred honor.

"'"4. *Resolved,* That as we now acknowledge the existence and control of no law or legal officer, civil or military, within this county, we do hereby ordain and adopt, as a rule of life, all, each and every of our former laws wherein, nevertheless, the Crown of Great Britain never can be considered as holding rights, privileges, immunities, or authority therein.

"'"5. *Resolved,* That it is also further decreed, that all, each and every military officer in this county, is hereby reinstated to his former command and authority, he acting conformably to these regulations. And that every member present of this delegation shall henceforth be a civil officer, viz., a Justice of the Peace, in the character of a *'Committee-man,'* to issue process, hear and determine all matters of controversy, according to said adopted laws, and to preserve peace, and union, and harmony, in said county,—and to use every exertion to spread the love of country and fire of freedom throughout America, until a more general and organized government be established in this province."

"'A number of by-laws were also added, merely to protect the association from confusion, and to regulate their general conduct as citizens. After sitting in the court-house all night, neither sleepy, hungry, nor fatigued, and after discussing every paragraph, they were all passed, sanctioned, and decreed *unanimously,* about 2 o'clock A. M., May 20. In a few days, a deputation of said delegation convened, when Capt. *James Jack,* of Charlotte, was deputed as express to the Congress at Philadelphia, with a copy of said Resolves and Proceedings, together with a letter addressed to our three representatives there, viz., *Richard Caswell, William Hooper and Joseph Hewes*—under express injunction, personally, and through the State representation, to use all possible means to have said proceedings sanctioned and approved by the General Congress. On the return of Captain Jack, the delegation learned that their proceedings were individually approved by the Members of Congress, but that it was deemed premature to lay them before the House. A joint letter from said three Members of Congress was also received, complimentary of the zeal in the common cause, and recommending perseverance, order and energy.

" 'The subsequent harmony, unanimity, and exertion in the cause of liberty and independence, evidently resulting from these regulations and the continued exertion of said delegation, apparently tranquillized this section of the State, and met with the concurrence and high approbation of the Council of Safety, who held their sessions at Newbern and Wilmington, alternately, and who confirmed the nomination and acts of the delegation in their official capacity.

" 'From this delegation originated the Court of Enquiry of this county, who constituted and held

Declaration of Independence

their first session in Charlotte—they then held their meetings regularly at Charlotte, at Col. James Harris's, and at Col. Phifer's, alternately, one week at each place. It was a Civil Court founded on military process. Before this Judicature, all suspicious persons were made to appear, who were formally tried and banished, or continued under guard. Its jurisdiction was as unlimited as toryism, and its decrees as final as the confidence and patriotism of the county. Several were arrested and brought before them from Lincoln, Rowan and the adjacent counties.

" '[The foregoing is a true copy of the papers on the above subject, left in my hands by John McKnitt Alexander, dec'd. I find it mentioned on file that the original book was burned April, 1800. That a copy of the proceedings was sent to Hugh Williamson, in New York, then writing a History of North Carolina, and that a copy was sent to Gen. W. R. Davie.

J. McKNITT.]

" 'STATE OF NORTH CAROLINA,
    Mecklenburg County.

" 'I, Samuel Henderson, do hereby certify, that the paper annexed was obtained by me from Maj. William Davie in its present situation, soon after the death of his father, Gen. William R. Davie, and given to Dr. Joseph McKnitt by me. In searching for some particular paper, I came across this, and, knowing the hand-writing of John McKnitt Alexander, took it up, and examined it. Maj. Davie said to me (when asked how it became torn) his sisters had torn it, not knowing what it was.

" 'Given under my hand, this 25th Nov., 1830.

" 'SAM. HENDERSON.'

"[NOTE.—To this certificate of Dr. Henderson is annexed the copy of the paper A, originally deposited by John McKnitt Alexander in the hands of *Gen. Davie,* whose name seems to have been mistaken by Mr. Jefferson for that of *Gov. Caswell.* See preface, pages 5 and 6. This paper is somewhat torn, but is entirely legible, and constitutes the 'solemn and positive proof of authenticity' which Mr. Jefferson required, and which would doubtless have been satisfactory had it been submitted to him.]

"LETTER FROM HON. C. TAIT, MEMBER OF CONGRESS FROM GEORGIA.

" 'WASHINGTON, Jan'y 25th, 1819.

" 'DEAR SIR:—Of late an inquiry, and in some instances a controversy, has arisen respecting the origin of the American Revolution. Some say it began in Virginia, and for this honor the Virginians strenuously contend. The people of New England assert that it commenced in the Town of Boston, and much has been written of late on the subject. This controversy has been dignified by a correspondence between two ex-Presidents of the U. S.—Adams and Jefferson. Other parts of the country begin to put in their pretensions to an early movem't in this great event, which is destined to influence the affairs of mankind. North Carolina thinks she has some claims in this regard; and Mr. Macon of the Senate is collecting what information he can on the subject. It appears by a document lately furnished him that the people of the county of Mecklenburg of that State, so early as on the 20th of May, 1775, declared themselves *independent* in due form in a convention at the town of Charlotte. That Adam or Abram Alexander was the President of this Convention, and that John McKnitt Alexander was its Secretary or Clerk. It also appears by this curious document that *Cap'n James Jack* was the person chosen to carry the proceedings of this convention to the Continental Congress sitting at Philadelphia. Presuming that the Cap'n Jack is no other person than your respected father, I informed Mr. Macon he is still living in the county of Elbert and State of Georgia. This information has produced a request from Mr. Macon that I would write to you and request it as a favor of you to forward to him any Document, or copy of a Document, which has any relation to the Mecklenburg Convention, or of the Revolutionary movements in that part of the country, at that early period. This I persuade myself you will with pleasure do. By possibility your father may have preserved, as a precious relic of those days, some papers relating to the proceedings alluded to, and in which he bore an honorable part. If this is the case it will gratify Mr. Macon very much to get them or a copy of them.

" 'Present my respects to Mrs. Jack, to your father and mother, and believe me,

" 'Yours, &c., &c.,
" '(Signed.)   C. Tait.
" 'Gen. P. Jack.
" 'P. S.—Mr. Macon will be very glad to hear from you before the adjournment of Congress; his given name is Nathaniel.   C. T.'

"CAPTAIN JACK'S CERTIFICATE.

" 'Having seen in the newspapers some pieces respecting the Declaration of Independence by the people of Mecklenburg County, in the State of North Carolina, in May, 1775, and being solicited to state what I know of that transaction; I would observe, that for some time previous to, and at the time those resolutions were agreed upon, I resided in the town of Charlotte, Mecklenburg County; was privy to a number of meetings of some of the most influential and leading characters of that county on the subject, before the final adoption of the resolutions—and at the time they were adopted; among those who appeared to take the lead, may be mentioned Hezekiah Alexander, who generally acted as Chairman, John McKnitt Alexander, as Secretary,

Abraham Alexander, Adam Alexander, Maj. John Davidson, Maj. (afterwards Gen.) Wm. Davidson, Col. Thomas Polk, Ezekiel Polk, Dr. Ephraim Brevard, Samuel Martin, Duncan Ochletree, William Willson, Robert Irvin.

" 'When the resolutions were finally agreed on, they were publicly proclaimed from the court-house door in the town of Charlotte, and received with every demonstration of joy by the inhabitants.

" 'I was then solicited to be the bearer of the proceedings to Congress. I set out the following month, say June, and in passing through Salisbury, the General Court was sitting—at the request of the court I handed a copy of the resolutions to Col. Kennon, an Attorney, and they were read aloud in open court. Major William Davidson, and Mr. Avery, an attorney, called on me at my lodgings the evening after, and observed, they had heard of but one person, (a Mr. Beard) but approved of them.

" 'I then proceeded on to Philadelphia, and delivered the Mecklenburg Declaration of Independence of May, 1775, to Richard Caswell and William Hooper, the Delegates to Congress from the State of North Carolina.

" 'I am now in the eighty-eighth year of my age, residing in the county of Elbert, in the State of Georgia. I was in the Revolutionary War, from the commencement to the close. I would further observe, that the Rev. Francis Cummins, a Presbyterian Clergyman, of Greene County, in this State, was a student in the town of Charlotte at the time of the adoption of the resolutions, and is as well, or perhaps better acquainted with the proceedings at that time, than any man now living.

"'Col. William Polk, of Raleigh, in North Carolina, was living with his father, Thomas, in Charlotte, at the time I have been speaking of, and although then too young to be forward in the business, yet the leading circumstances I have related cannot have escaped his recollection.

"'JAMES JACK.

"'Signed this 7th Dec., 1819, in presence of
"'JOB WESTON, C. C. O.
JAMES OLIVER, Atto. at Law.'

"C 2.

"'NORTH CAROLINA,
Cabarrus County, Nov. 29, 1830.

"'We, the undersigned, do hereby certify that w have frequently heard William S. Alexander, dec'd say that he, the said Wm. S. Alexander, was a Philadelphia, on mercantile business, in the earl part of the summer of 1775, say in June; and tha on the day that Gen. Washington left Philadelphi to take the command of the Northern army, he, th said Wm. S. Alexander, met with Capt. James Jack who informed him, the said William S. Alexander that he, the said James Jack, was there as the agent c bearer of the Declaration of Independence made i

Declaration of Independence

Charlotte, on the twentieth day of May, seventeen hundred and seventy-five, by the citizens of Mecklenburg, then including Cabarrus, with instructions to present the same to the Delegates from North Carolina, and by them to be laid before Congress, and which he said he had done; in which Declaration the aforesaid citizens of Mecklenburg renounced their allegiance to the crown of Great Britain, and set up a government for themselves, under the title of the Committee of Safety.

" 'Given under our hands the date above written.

" 'ALPHONSO ALEXANDER,
AMOS ALEXANDER.
J. McKNITT.'

"D.

" '*Lexington, (Georgia,) November* 10, 1819.

" 'DEAR SIR:—The bearer, the Hon. Thomas W. Cobb, has suggested to me that you had a desire to know something particularly of the proceedings of the citizens of Mecklenburg County, in North Carolina, about the beginning of our Revolutionary War.

" 'Previous to my becoming more particular, I will suppose you remember the Regulation business, which took its rise in or before the year 1770, and issued and ended in a battle between the Regulators and Governor Tryon, in the spring of 1771. Some of the Regulators were killed, and the whole dispersed. The Regulators' conduct "was a *rudis indigestaque moles,*" as Ovid says, about the beginning of creation; but the embryotic principles of the Revolution were in their temper and views. They wanted strength, consistency, a Congress and a Washington at their head. Tryon sent his officers and minions through the State, and imposed the oath of allegiance upon the people, even as far up as Mecklenburg County. In the year 1775, after our Revolution began, the principal characters of Mecklenburg County met on two sundry days, in Queen's Museum in Charlotte, to digest articles for a State Constitution, in anticipation that the Province would proceed to do so. In this business the leading characters were, the Rev. Hezekiah James Balch, a graduate of Princeton College, an elegant scholar; Waightstill Avery, Esq., Attorney at Law; Hezekiah and John McKnitt Alexander, Esqrs., Col. Thomas Polk, etc., etc.

" 'Many men, and young men, (myself one,) before magistrates, abjured allegiance to George III., or any other foreign power. At length, in the same year 1775, I think at least positively before July 4th, 1776, the males generally of that county met on a certain day in Charlotte, and from the head of the court-house stairs proclaimed Independence of English Government, by their herald Col. Thomas Polk. I was present, and saw and heard it, and as a young man, and then a student in Queen's Museum, was an agent in these things. I did not then take and keep the dates, and cannot, as to date, be so particular as I could wish. Capt. James Jack, then of Charlotte,

Declaration of Independence 183

but now of Elbert County, in Georgia, was sent with the account of these proceedings to Congress, then in Philadelphia—and brought back to the county, the thanks of Congress for their zeal—and the advice of Congress to be a little more patient, until Congress should take the measures thought to be best.

" 'I would suppose, sir, that some minutes of these things must be found among the records of the first Congress, that would perfectly settle their dates. I am perfectly sure, being present at the whole of them, they were before our National Declaration of Independence.

" 'Hon. Sir, if the above few things can afford you any gratification, it will add to the happiness of your friend and humble servant.

" 'FRANCIS CUMMINS.

" 'HON. NATHANIEL MACON.'

"E.

" '*Vesuvius Furnace, 4th October,* 1830.

" 'DEAR SIR,—Agreeably to your request, I will give you the details of the Mecklenburg Declaration of Independence on the 20th of May, 1775, as well as I can recollect after a lapse of fifty-five years. I was then a lad about half grown, was present on that occasion (a looker on).

"'During the winter and spring preceding that event, several popular meetings of the people were held in Charlotte; two of which I attended.—Papers were read, grievances stated, and public measures discussed. As printing was not then common in the South, the papers were mostly manuscript; one or more of which was from the pen of the Reverend Doctor Reese, (then of Mecklenburg,) which met with general approbation, and copies of it circulated. It is to be regretted that those and other papers published at that period, and the journal of their proceedings, are lost.—They would show much of the spirit and tone of thinking which prepared them for the measures they afterwards adopted.

"'On the 20th of May, 1775, besides the two persons elected from each militia company, (usually called Committee-men,) a much larger number of citizens attended in Charlotte than at any former meeting—perhaps half the men in the county. The news of the battle of Lexington, the 19th of April preceding, had arrived. There appeared among the people much excitement. The committee were organized in the Court-house by appointing Abraham Alexander, Esq., Chairman, and John McKnitt Alexander, Esq., Clerk or Secretary to the meeting.

"'After reading a number of papers as usual, and much animated discussion, the question was taken, and they resolved to declare themselves independent. One among other reasons offered, that the King or Ministry had, by proclamation or some edict, declared the Colonies out of the protection of the British Crown; they ought, therefore, to declare themselves out of his protection, and resolve on independence. That their proceedings might be in due form, a sub-committee, consisting of Doctor Ephraim Brevard, a Mr. Kennon, an attorney, and a third person, whom I do not recollect, were appointed to draft their Declaration. They retired from the court-house for some time; but the committee continued in session in it. One circumstance occurred I distinctly remember: A member of the committee, who had said but little before, addressed the Chairman as follows: "If you resolve on independence, how shall we all be absolved from the obligations of the oath we took to be true to King George the 3d about four years ago, after the Regulation battle, when we were sworn whole militia companies together. I should be glad to know how gentlemen can clear their consciences after taking that oath." This speech produced confusion. The Chairman could scarcely preserve order, so many wished to reply. There appeared great indignation and contempt at the speech of the member. Some said it was nonsense; others that allegiance and protection were reciprocal; when protection was withdrawn, allegiance ceased; that the oath was only binding while the King protected us in the enjoyment of our rights and liberties as they existed at the time it was taken; which he had not done, but now declared us out of his protection; therefore was not binding. Any man who interpreted it otherwise, was a fool. By way of illustration, (pointing to a green tree near the court-house,) stated, if he was sworn to do anything as long as the leaves continued on that tree, it was so long binding; but when the leaves fell, he was discharged from its obligation. This was said to be certainly applicable in the present case. Out of respect for a worthy citizen, long since deceased, and his respectable connections, I forbear to mention names; for, though he was a friend to the cause, a suspicion rested on him in the public mind for some time after.

" 'The sub-committee appointed to draft the resolutions returned, and Doctor Ephraim Brevard read their report, as near as I can recollect, in the very words we have since seen them several times in print. It was unanimously adopted, and shortly after it was moved and seconded to have proclamation made and the people collected, that the proceedings be read at the Court-house door, in order that all might hear them. It was done, and they were received with enthusiasm. It was then proposed by some one aloud to give three cheers and throw up their hats. It was immediately adopted, and the hats thrown. Several of them lit on the court-house roof. The owners had some difficulty to reclaim them.

" 'The foregoing is all from personal knowledge. I understood afterwards that Captain James Jack, then of Charlotte, undertook, on the request of the committee, to carry a copy of their proceedings to Congress, which then sat in Philadelphia; and on his way, at Salisbury, the time of court, Mr. Kennon, who was one of the committee who assisted in drawing the Declaration, prevailed on Captain Jack to get his papers, and have them read publicly;

which was done, and the proceedings met with general approbation. But two of the Lawyers, John Dunn and a Mr. Booth, dissented, and asserted they were treasonable, and endeavored to have Captain Jack detained. He drew his pistols, and threatened to kill the first man who would interrupt him, and passed on. The news of this reached Charlotte in a short time after, and the executive of the committee, whom they had invested with suitable powers, ordered a party of ten or twelve armed horsemen to bring said Lawyers from Salisbury; when they were brought, and the case investigated before the committee. Dunn, on giving security and making fair promises, was permitted to return, and Booth was sentenced to go to Camden, in South Carolina, out of the sphere of his influence. My brother George Graham and the late Col. John Carruth were of the party that went to Salisbury; and it is distinctly remembered that when in Charlotte they came home at night, in order to provide for their trip to Camden; and that they and two others of the party took Booth to that place. This was the first military expedition from Mecklenburg in the Revolutionary War, and believed to be the first anywhere to the South.

" 'Yours respectfully,

" 'J. Graham.

" 'Dr. Jos. McKt. Alexander,

" 'Mecklenburg, N. Carolina.'

"F.

"EXTRACT FROM THE MEMOIR OF THE LATE REV. HUMPHREY HUNTER.

"'Orders were presently issued by Col. Thos. Polk to the several militia companies, that two men, selected from each corps, should meet at the courthouse on the 19th of May, 1775, in order to consult with each other upon such measures as might be thought best to be pursued. Accordingly, on said day a far larger number than two out of each company were present. There was some difficulty in choosing the commissioners. To have chosen all thought to be worthy, would have rendered the meeting too numerous. The following were selected, and styled Delegates, and are here given, according to my best recollection, as they were placed on roll: Abram Alexander, sen'r, Thomas Polk, Rich'd Harris, sen'r, Adam Alexander, Richard Barry, John McKnitt Alexander, Neil Morison, Hezekiah Alexander, Hezekiah J. Balch, Zacheus Wilson, John Phifer, James Harris, William Kennon, John Ford, Henry Downs, Ezra Alexander, William Graham, John Queary, Chas. Alexander, Waightstill Avery, Ephraim Brevard, Benjamin Patton, Matthew McClure, Robert Irwin, John Flenniken and David Reese.

"'Abram Alexander was nominated, and unanimously voted to the Chair. John McKnitt Alexander and Ephraim Brevard were chosen Secretaries. The Chair being occupied, and the Clerks seated, the

House was called to order and proceeded to business. Then a full, a free, and dispassionate discussion obtained on the various subjects for which the delegation had been convened, and the following resotions were unanimously ordained:

"'1st. *Resolved,* That whosoever directly or indirectly abetted, or in any way, form or manner, countenanced the unchartered and dangerous invasion of our rights, as claimed by Great Britain, is an enemy to this country, to America, and to the inherent and inalienable rights of man.

"'2d. *Resolved,* That we, the citizens of Mecklenburg County, do hereby dissolve the political bands which have connected· us to the mother country, and hereby absolve ourselves from all allegiance to the British Crown, and abjure all political connection, contract, or association, with that nation, who have wantonly trampled on our rights and liberties and inhumanly shed the blood of American patriots at Lexington.

"'3d. *Resolved,* That we do hereby declare ourselves a free and independent people; are, and of right ought to be, a sovereign and self-governing Association, under the control of no power other than that of our God and the general government of the Congress; to the maintenance of which independence, we solemnly pledge to each other our mutual co-operation, our lives, our fortunes, and our most sacred honor.

"'4th. *Resolved,* That as we now acknowledge the existence and control of no law or legal officer, civil or military, within this county, we do hereby ordain and adopt as a rule of life, all, each and every of our former laws—wherein, nevertheless, the crown of Great Britain never can be considered as holding rights, privileges, immunities or authority therein.

" '5th. *Resolved,* That it is further decreed, that all, each and every military officer in this county, is hereby reinstated in his former command and authority, he acting conformably to these regulations. And that every member present, of this delegation, shall henceforth be a civil officer, viz., a Justice of the Peace, in the character of a *"Committeeman,"* to issue process, hear and determine all matters of controversy, according to said adopted laws, and to preserve peace, union and harmony in said county;—and to use every exertion to spread the love of country and fire of freedom throughout America, until a more general and organized government be established in this province.

" 'Those resolves having been concurred in, byelaws and regulations for the government of a standing Committee of Public Safety were enacted and acknowledged. Then a select committee was appointed, to report on the ensuing day a full and definite statement of grievances, together with a more correct and formal draft of the Declaration of Independence. The proceedings having been thus arranged and somewhat in readiness for promulgation, the Delegation then adjourned until to-morrow, at 12 o'clock.

" 'The 20th of May, at 12 o'clock, the Delegation, as above, had convened. The select committee were

Declaration of Independence 191

also present, and reported agreeably to instructions, viz., a statement of grievances and formal draft of the Declaration of Independence, written by Ephraim Brevard, chairman of said committee, and read by him to the Delegation. The resolves, byelaws and regulations were read by John McKnitt Alexander. It was then announced from the Chair, Are you all agreed? There was not a dissenting voice. Finally, the whole proceedings were read distinctly and audibly, at the court-house door, by Col. Thomas Polk, to a large, respectable and approving assemblage of citizens, who were present, and gave sanction to the business of the day. A copy of all those transactions were then drawn off, and given in charge to Capt. James Jack, then of Charlotte, that he should present them to Congress, then in session in Philadelphia.

" 'On that memorable day I was 20 years and 14 days of age, a very deeply interested spectator, recollecting the dire hand of oppression that had driven me from my native clime, now pursuing me in this happy asylum, and seeking to bind again in the fetters of bondage.

" 'On the return of Capt. Jack, he reported that Congress, individually, manifested their entire approbation of the conduct of the Mecklenburg citizens; but deemed it premature to lay them officially before the House.'

["Note.—The foregoing extract is copied from a manuscript account of the Revolutionary War in the South, addressed by the writer to a friend, who had requested historical information upon the subject. Mr. Hunter was in the battle of Camden, and has given an interesting narrative of the circumstances connected with the death of Baron DeKalb. The manuscript gives the biography of the writer, from which it appears he was a native of Ireland, and born on the 14th of May, 1755, and at an early age emigrated from his native land to the Province of North Carolina.]

"ADDITIONAL PAPERS NOT PARTICULARLY REFERRED TO IN THE PREFACE.

"From the *Raleigh Register,* of February 18, 1820.

"'MECKLENBURG DECLARATION OF INDEPENDENCE.

"'When this Declaration was first published in April last, some doubts were expressed in the Eastern papers as to its authenticity, (none of the Histories of the Revolution having noticed the circumstance.) Col. William Polk, of this City, (who, though a mere youth at the time, was present at the meeting which made the Declaration, and whose Father, being Colonel of the county, appears to have acted a conspicuous part on the occasion,) observing this, assured us of the correctness of the facts generally, though he thought there were errors as to the name of the Secretary, etc., and said that he should probably be able to correct these, and throw some further light on the subject, by inquiries amongst some of his old friends in Mecklenburg County. He has accordingly made inquiries, and communicated to us the following Documents as the result, which, we presume, will do away with all doubts on the subject.

" 'CERTIFICATE.

" 'STATE OF NORTH CAROLINA,
Mecklenburg County.

" 'At the request of Col. William Polk, of Raleigh, made to Major-General George Graham, soliciting him to procure all the information that could be obtained at this late period, of the transactions which took place in the county of Mecklenburg, in the year 1775, as it respected the people of that county having declared Independence; of the time when the Declaration was made; who were the principal movers and leaders, and the members who composed the body of Patriots who made the Declaration, and signed the same.

" 'We, the undersigned citizens of the said county, and of the several ages set forth opposite to each of our names, do certify, and on our honor declare, that we were present in the town of Charlotte, in the said county of Mecklenburg, on the 19th day of May, 1775, when two persons elected from each Captain's Company in said county, appeared as Delegates, to take into consideration the state of the country, and to adopt such measures as to them seemed best, to secure their lives, liberty, and property, from the storm which was gathering, and had burst upon their fellow-citizens to the Eastward, by a British Army, under the authority of the British King and Parliament.

"'The order for the election of Delegates was given by Col. Thomas Polk, the commanding officer of the militia of the county, with a request that their powers should be ample, touching any measure that should be proposed.

"'We do further certify and declare, that to the best of our recollection and belief, the delegation was complete from every company, and that the meeting took place in the court-house, about 12 o'clock on the said 19th day of May, 1775, when *Abraham Alexander* was chosen Chairman, and Dr. *Ephraim Brevard,* Secretary. That the Delegates continued in session until in the night of that day; that on the 20th they again met, when a committee, under the direction of the Delegates, had formed several resolves, which were read, and which went to declare themselves, and the people of Mecklenburg County, Free and Independent of the King and Parliament of Great Britain—and that, from that day thenceforth, all allegiance and political relation was absolved between the good people of Mecklenburg and the King of Great Britain; which Declaration was signed by every member of the Delegation, under the shouts and huzzas of a very large assembly of the people of the county, who had come to know the issue of the meeting. We further believe, that the Declaration of Independence was drawn up by the Secretary, Dr. Ephraim Brevard, and that it was conceived and brought about through the instrumentality and popularity of Col. Thomas Polk, Abraham Alexander, John McKnitt Alexander, Adam Alexander, Ephraim Brevard, John Phifer, and Hezekiah Alexander, with some others.

" 'We do further certify and declare, that in a few days after the Delegates adjourned, Capt. James Jack, of the town of Charlotte, was engaged to carry the resolves to the President of Congress, and to our Representatives—one copy for each; and that his expenses were paid by a voluntary subscription. And we do know that Captain Jack executed the trust, and returned with answers, both from the President and our Delegates in Congress, expressive of their entire approbation of the course that had been adopted, recommending a continuance in the same; and that the time would soon be, when the whole Continent would follow our example.

" 'We further certify and declare, that the measures which were adopted at the time before mentioned, had a general influence on the people of this county to unite them in the cause of liberty and the country, at that time; that the same unanimity and patriotism continued unimpaired to the close of the war; and that the resolutions had considerable effect in harmonizing the people in two or three adjoining counties.

" 'That a committee of Safety for the county were elected, who were clothed with civil and military power, and under their authority several disaffected persons in Rowan, and Tryon (now Lincoln County,) were sent for, examined, and conveyed (after it was satisfactorily proven they were inimical) to Camden, in South Carolina, for safe-keeping.

" 'We do further certify, that the acts passed by the Committee of Safety, were received as the Civil Law of the land in many cases, and that Courts of Justice for the decision of controversies between the people were held, and we have no recollection that dissatisfaction existed in any instance with regard to the judgments of said courts.

" 'We are not, at this late period, able to give the names of all the Delegation who formed the Declaration of Independence; but can safely declare as to the following persons being of the number, viz: Thomas Polk, Abraham Alexander, John McKnitt Alexander, Adam Alexander, Ephraim Brevard, John Phifer, Hezekiah James Balch, Benjamin Patton, Hezekiah Alexander, Richard Barry, William Graham, Matthew McClure, Robert Irwin, Zacheus Wilson, Neil Morrison, John Flenniken, John Queary, Ezra Alexander.

" 'In testimony of all and every part herein set forth, we have hereunto set our hands.

      " 'GEORGE GRAHAM, aged 61, near 62.
      " 'WILLIAM HUTCHISON, 68.
      " 'JONAS CLARK,   61.
      " 'ROBERT ROBINSON, 68.'

Declaration of Independence

"FROM JOHN SIMESON TO COL. WILLIAM POLK.

" '*Providence, January* 20, 1820.

" 'DEAR SIR,—After considerable delay, occasioned partly to obtain what information I could, in addition to my own knowledge of the facts in relation to our Declaration of Independence, and partly by a precarious, feeble old age, I now write to you in answer to yours of the 24th ult.

" 'I have conversed with many of my old friends and others, and all agree in the point, but few can state the particulars; for although our county is renowned for general intelligence, we have still some that don't read the public prints. You know, in the language of the day, every Province had its Congress, and Mecklenburg had its county Congress, as legally chosen as any other, and assumed an attitude until then without a precedent; but, alas! those worthies who conceived and executed that bold measure, are no more; and one reason why so little new light can be thrown on an old truth, may be this—and I appeal to yourself for the correctness of the remark—we who are now called Revolutionary men, were then thoughtless, precipitate youths; we cared not who conceived the bold act, our business was to adopt and support it. Yourself, sir, in your eighteenth year and on the spot, your worthy father, the most popular and influential character in the county, and yet you cannot state much from recollection. Your father, as commanding officer of the county, issued orders to the Captains to appoint two men from each company to represent them in the committee.—It was done. Neill Morrison, John Flenniken, from this company; Charles Alexander, John McKnitt Alexander, Hezekiah Alexander, Abraham Alexander, Esq., John Phifer, David Reese, Adam Alexander, Dickey Barry, John Queary, with others, whose names I cannot obtain. As to the names of those who drew up the Declaration, I am inclined to think Doctor Brevard was the principal, from his known talents in composition. It was, however, in substance and form, like that great national act agreed on thirteen months after. Ours was towards the close of May, 1775. In addition to what I have said, the same committee appointed three men to secure all the military stores for the county's use—Thomas Polk, John Phifer, and Joseph Kennedy. I was under arms near the head of the line, near Colonel Polk, and heard him distinctly read a long string of Grievances, the Declaration and Military Order above. I likewise heard Colonel Polk have two warm disputes with two men of the county, who said the measures were rash and unnecessary. He was applauded and they silenced. I was then in my 22d year, an enemy to usurpation and tyranny of every kind, with a retentive memory, and fond of liberty, that had a doubt arisen in my mind that the act would be controverted, proof would not have been wanting; but I comfort myself that none but the self-important peace-party and bluelights of the East, will have the assurance to oppose it any further. The biographer of Patrick Henry (Mr. Wirt) says he first suggested

Independence in the Virginia Convention; but it is known they did not reduce it to action—so that it will pass for nothing. The Courts likewise acted independently. I myself heard a dispute take place on the bench, and an acting magistrate was actually taken and sent to prison by an order of the Chairman.

" 'Thus, sir, have I thrown together all that I can at this time. I am too blind to write fair, and too old to write much sense—but if my deposition before the Supreme Court of the United States would add more weight to a truth so well known here, it should be at the service of my fellow-citizens of the county and State generally.

" 'I am, sir, your friend and humble servant,

" 'JOHN SIMESON, Sen.

" 'P. S.—I will give you a short anecdote. An aged man near me, on being asked if he knew anything of this affair, replied, *"Och, aye,* TAM POLK *declared Independence long before any body else."* This old man is 81.'

"CERTIFICATE OF ISAAC ALEXANDER.

" 'I hereby certify that I was present in Charlotte on the 19th and 20th days of May, 1775, when a regular deputation from all the Captains' companies of militia in the county of Mecklenburg, to wit: Col. Thomas Polk, Adam Alexander, Lieut.-Col. Abram

Alexander, John McKnitt Alexander, Hezekiah Alexander, Ephraim Brevard, and a number of others, who met to consult and take measures for the peace and tranquillity of the citizens of said county, and who appointed Abraham Alexander their Chairman, and Doctor Ephraim Brevard, Secretary; who, after due consultation, declared themselves absolved from their allegiance to the King of Great Britain, and drew up a Declaration of their Independence, which was unanimously adopted; and employed Capt. James Jack to carry copies thereof to Congress, who accordingly went. These are a part of the transactions that took place at that time, as far as my recollection serves me.

" 'Isaac Alexander.
" 'October 8, 1830.'

"Certificate of Samuel Wilson.

" 'State of North Carolina,
  Mecklenburg County.

" 'I do hereby certify, that in May, 1775, a committee or delegation from the different militia companies in this county met in Charlotte; and after consulting together, they publicly declared their independence on Great Britain, and on her Government. This was done before a large collection of people, who highly approved of it. I was then and there present, and heard it read from the courthouse door. Certified by me,
" 'Samuel Wilson.'

"CERTIFICATE OF JOHN DAVIDSON.

" '*Beaver Dam, October* 5, 1830.

" 'DEAR SIR:—I received your note of the 25th of last month, requiring information relative to the Mecklenburg Declaration of Independence. As I am, perhaps, the only person living, who was a member of that Convention, and being far advanced in years, and not having my mind frequently directed to that circumstance for some years, I can give you but a very succinct history of that transaction. There were two men chosen from each captain's company, to meet in Charlotte, to take the subject into consideration. John McKnitt Alexander and myself were chosen from one company; and many other members were there that I now recollect, whose names I deem unnecessary to mention. When the members met, and were perfectly organized for business, a motion was made to declare ourselves independent of the Crown of Great Britain, which was carried by a large majority. Dr. Ephraim Brevard was then appointed to give us a sketch of the Declaration of Independence, which he did. James Jack was appointed to take it on to the American Congress, then sitting in Philadelphia, with particular instructions to deliver it to the North Carolina Delegation in Congress, (Hooper and Caswell.) When Jack returned, he stated that the Declaration was presented to Congress, and the reply was, that they highly esteemed the patriotism of the citizens of Mecklenburg; but they thought the measure too premature.

"'I am confident that the Declaration of Independence by the people of Mecklenburg was made public at least twelve months before that of the Congress of the United States.

"'I do certify that the foregoing statement, relative to the Mecklenburg Independence is correct, and which I am willing to be qualified to, should it be required.

"'Yours respectfully,
"'JOHN DAVIDSON.
"'Doct. J. M. ALEXANDER.'

"NOTE.—The following is a copy of an original paper furnished by the writer of the foregoing certificate, from which it would seem, that, from the period of the Mecklenburg Declaration, every individual friendly to the American cause was furnished by the *Chairman of that meeting,* ABRAM ALEXANDER, with testimonials of the character he had assumed; and in this point of view the paper affords strong collateral testimony of the correctness of many of the foregoing certificates:

"'NORTH CAROLINA, Mecklenburg County,

November 28, 1775.

"'These may certify to all whom they may concern, that the bearer hereof, William Henderson, is

allowed here to be a true friend to liberty, and signed the Association.
" 'Certified by
" 'Abr'm Alexander, *Chairman*
" '*of the Committee of P. S.*'

"Letter from J. G. M. Ramsey.

" '*Mecklenburg, T. Oct.* 1, 1830.
" 'Dear Sir:—Yours of 21st ultimo was duly received. In answer I have only to say, that little is in my possession on the subject alluded to which you have not already seen. Subjoined are the certificates of two gentlemen of this county, whose respectability and veracity are attested by their acquaintances here, as well as by the accompanying testimonials of the magistrates in whose neighborhood they reside. With this you will also receive extracts from letters on the same subject from gentlemen well known to you, and to the country at large.
" 'I am, very respectfully, yours, &c.,
" 'J. G. M. Ramsey.'

"Certificate of James Johnson.

" 'I, James Johnson, now of Knox County, Tennessee, but formely of Mecklenburg County, North Carolina, do hereby certify, that to the best of my recollection, in the month of May, 1775, there were several meetings in Charlotte concerning the impending war. Being young, I was not called on to take an active part in the same; but one thing I do positively remember, that she (Mecklenburg County) did meet and hold a Convention, declared independence, and sent a man to Philadelphia with the proceedings. And I do further certify, that I am well acquainted with several of the men who formed or constituted said Convention, viz.: John McKnitt Alexander, Hezekiah Alexander, Abraham Alexander, Adam Alexander, Robert Irwin, Neill Morrison, John Flenniken, John Queary.

" 'Certified by me this 11th day of October, 1827.

" 'JAMES JOHNSON,

" 'In my seventy-third year.'

"CERTIFICATE OF ELIJAH JOHNSON AND JAMES WILHITE.

" 'We, Elijah Johnson and James Wilhite, acting Justices of the Peace for the county of Knox, do certify, that we have been a long time well acquainted with Samuel Montgomery and James Johnson, both residents of Knox County; and that they are entitled to full credit, and any statement they may make to implicit confidence.

" 'Given under our hands and seals this 4th day of October, 1830.

"'ELIJAH JOHNSON, (Seal.)
"'JAMES WILHITE, (Seal.)
"'Justices of the Peace for Knox County.'

"NOTE.—Mr. Montgomery's certificate does not purport to state the facts as having come under his own personal observation. It is therefore omitted in this publication."

INDEX

----, Charles 99 Devil
Charley 98
ADAMS, 176 John 17
152 Mr 157
ALEXANDER, 62 119
Abigail Bane 114
Abr'm 203 Abraham
35 100 102 138 168
172 179 184 194-
196 198 200 204
Abram 177 200 202
Abram Sr 188 Adam
76 100 107-109 135
167 177 179 188
195-196 198-199
204 Alphonso 181
Amos 181 Charles
100 109-110 132
167 198 Chas 188
Dan 101 Dorcas 102

ALEXANDER (Cont.)
Elias 102 Elizabeth
102 Evan 109 166
Ezra 100 124 168
188 196 Hezekiah
100 102 112 116
125 138 167 178
182 188 195-196
198 200 204 Isaac
102 109-110 199-
200 J M 202 James
112 Jane 112
Jemima 112 Jno
Mcknitt 167 Joab
102 John M'knitt
111 John Mcknitt
15-19 22 24-25 27-
28 32 34 37 49 61
79-80 100 105-106
112 116 134 159

ALEXANDER (Cont.)
161 168 172 175-
178 182 184 188
191 195-196 198
200-201 204 Jos
Mckt 187 Joseph
Mcknitt 17 37 49
114 M Winslow 135
Margaret 100 112
Mary 109-110 Mr
113 153 157-158
163 Nathaniel 20
100 102 Stephen
117 Thomas 101 121
William 32 102 107
William Bane 114
William S 180 Wm
101 Zebulon 110
APPLETON, 58
ARMSTRONG, Col 111
ARNOLD, 94
ASHE, Gov 147 John
64 Samuel 65
AVERY, 126 James 125
Mr 179 Waighstill
182 Waightstill 115
125 130 161 168
188
BALCH, Anne 115
Hezekiah 114-115
Hezekiah J 167 188

BALCH (Cont.)
Hezekiah James 47
182 196 Hezekiah
Jones 10 James
115-116 John 114
Steven B 116
William 116
BALTIMORE, Lord 87
BANCROFT, 104 George
30 Mr 22 43
BANE, Jane 112
BARRY, Anne 121
Dickey 198 Mr 122
Richard 121 168 188
196
BEARD, Mr 179
BIGGLESTON, Mr 73
BOOTE, 72-73
BOOTH, Mr 187
BOOTHE, 142
BOWDITCH, Mr 155
BRADLEY, 143 Frank
145
BRAGG, John 166
BREVARD, 104 106
126 Adam 30-31 Dr
28 46-47 53 56 113
198 Eph 43 Ephraim
10-11 20 27 99 103
167 179 185-186
188 191 194-196

INDEX   209

BREVARD (Cont.)
    200-201 Jane 103
    John 103 Margaret
    99 Robert 103
    Zebulon 103
BROCK, R A 128
BROWN, 100
BROWNFIELD, John
    125
BRYAN, 125 145
BURKE, Mr 78
BUTLER, 106
CALDWELL, Abigail
    Bane 114 Dr 109 Mr
    35 S C 114 Samuel
    C 34
CAMPBELL, 93
    Farquard 73-74
CAPPLES, William 104
CARR, Robert Sr 144
CARRUTH, John 187
CASWELL, 21 91 154
    157 159-160 201
    Gov 176 Mr 13 158
    Richard 20 73 174
    179
CAWELL, 153
CHARLES I, 86
CLARK, Jonas 50 62
    196
CLARKE, 92

CLEVELAND, 93
COBB, Thomas W 181
CONGER, John 118
    Lizzie 118
CORNWALLIS, 93 96
    106 113 122 135
    137 142 Lord 140
COULSON, John 74
CROMWELL, 86
CUMMINGS, Francis
    139
CUMMINS, Francis 160
    179 183
DARTMOUTH, Earl 55
    58 65
DAVIDSON, Benjamin
    Wilson 36 Gen 96
    113 140 John 34-35
    76 81 112 134 137
    168 179 201-202
    Joseph 36 Maj 135
    Mary 134 Robert 134
    Robert F 35 Violet
    134 W L 125 W Lee
    136 William Lee 92
    Wm 179
DAVIE, 17-18 22 29 33-
    34 37 80 121 158
    172 Maj 176 W R
    159 William R 16 95
    175

DEKALB, Baron 192
DENNIS, Littleton 125
DICKERSON, 106
   James Polk 106
DICKINSON, 154
DICKSON, John 145
   Thomas 145
DOWNS, Henry 130-
   131 168 188 Samuel
   131 Thomas 131
DOYLE, Maj 142 144
DRAPER, 84 Lyman 28
   30 43 58-59
DUNN, 72-73 142 John
   187
ELLSWORTH, Chief
   Justice 115
FERGUSON, Col 93
FLENNIKEN, John 168
   188 196 198 204
FLENNIKIN, David 122
   James 122 John 122
FOARD, John 131
FOOTE, 100 117 131
   133 Dr 106 111
FOR, John 168
FORCE, Peter 43 59
FORD, John 188
FRANKLIN, Dr 113
GARDEN, 29-30 52
   Alexander 26

GARDEN (Cont.)
   Maj 27-28 36 51 81
GATES, 94 121 137
GEORGE III, King 15 31
   63 65 76 182 185
   King 32
GIRARDIN, 154
GOODWINE, Anne 115
GRAHAM, 141
   Alexander 9 Gen 97
   George 19-20 50 62
   142 145 187 193
   196 J 187 John 105
   Joseph 19 49 135
   140 142 145 160
   William 123 168 188
   196
GREENE, Gen 26 94-95
   97 113 138 Nathan
   96
GREENWOOD, Mr 152
GRIDSBY, 105
HARNETT, Cornelius 65
   Mr 77
HARRIS, Charles 132-
   133 James 20 128
   132 167 175 188
   Matthew 118 Rich'd
   Sr 188 Richard 133
   Richard Sr 133 168
   Robert 32 118

HARRIS (Cont.)
128-129 133 Robert
Sr 132 Samuel 118
129 132 Thomas 132
W S 128 130 132-133
HAWKS, Dr 29 Francis
L 24 58
HENDERSON, Dr 121
159 Sam 176
Samuel 175 William
202
HENRY, James 145
Louis D 166 Mr 154
Patrick 198
HEWES, 17 21 153-154
157 159-160 Joseph
73 174 Mr 13 158
HOOPER, 17 21 153-154 157 159-160
201 Mr 13 158
William 68 73 174
179
HOPEWELL, 106
HORRY, 153
HOUSTON, Margaret
137
HOWE, Robert 65
HUBBARD, F M 126
HUNTER, 23 C L 125
Humphrey 50 133

HUNTER (Cont.)
160 188 Mr 192
HUTCHINSON, William
196
HUTCHISON, William
50 62
INDEPENDENCE,
Thomas 36
IRVIN, Robert 179
IRWIN, Col 123 129
Gen 111 John 110
Mary 110 Robert 20
110 161 168 188
196 204 William 110
JACK, Capt 13 20 61
72 136 138 142 159
187 James 12 23 62
137 174 177 180
182 186 191 195
200-201 Margaret
137 Mrs 178 P 178
JACKSON, Andrew 139
JAMES I, 86
JEFFERSON, 67 74 177
Mr 21-22 33 44-45
51 62-63 81-82 152
156 158-160 163
176 Th 155 Thomas
17 37 58 80
JOHNSON, Dr 89 95 98
Elijah 204-205

JOHNSON (Cont.)
  Gabriel 147 Gov 147
  James 203-204
  Joseph 43
JOHNSTON, Samuel 66
JONES, 112 126 154
  Allen 78 J Seawall
  60 Thomas 78
KASCIUS, Col 95
KENNEDY, Joseph 42
  50 198
KENNON, 126 Col 179
  Elizabeth 127 Mr 13
  185-186 Richard
  127 Richard Jr 127
  Robert 127 William
  10 47 127-128 167
  188
KILPATRICK, 51
KINCHEN, Mr 78
KING, R H 106
KNOX, Joanna 87
LEE, 26 Richard Henry
  45 82
LILLINGTON, 91
LONG, John 145
LOSSING, 136
M'CLURE, Matthew 123
MACON, Mr 177
  Nathaniel 160 178
  183
MADISON, Mr 148
MARSHALL, 154
MARTIN, 14-15 22 24
  26 28-30 33-34 36
  46-47 53 80-83 90
  146 Alexander 93
  Francois Xavia 19
  Gov 74 89 Judge 23
  25 51 69 Luther 115
  Mr 20-21 Samuel
  136 179
MCCLURE, Matthew
  123-124 168 188
  196 Thomas 145
MCCOMBS, Samuel
  143
MCDONALD, Gen 69
MCKNITT, 103 155 J
  181 John 112
  Joseph 152 175
  Margaret 112
MCNEIL, 97
MCNEILL, Alex 166
MCWHIRTER, Alex 103
  Jane 103
MCWHORTER, 116
MEANS, Miss 110
MONTGOMERY, Mr 205
  Samuel 204
MOORE, Col 69-70 Gen
  91

MORGAN, 113 N H 119
  N R 133 Nicholson
  Ross 118
MORISON, Neil 188
MORRISON, Alexander
  121 James 120-121
  Neil 120 168 196
  Neill 198 204
  William 120-121
MUIRHEAD, 84-85
NASH, Abner 64-65
  Francis 92 Gov 96
  Mr 78
OCHILTREE, Duncan
  113 136
OCHLETREE, Duncan
  179
OLIVER, James 180
OSBORNE, Adlai 104
PATTON, Benjamin 168
  188 196
PENN, 154 John 68
PERSON, Mr 78
PHIFER, Col 111 175
  John 50 76 161 167
  188 195-196 198
  Lieut 135 Martin 112
PHILLIPS, Charles 22
POLK, 84 86 Charles
  131 Col 91-93 95-96
  99 105 108-109 135

POLK (Cont.)
  137 Ezekiel 129 134
  136-137 179 Gen
  97-98 100 138
  James K 137 Joanna
  87 John 87
  Magdalene 84
  Margaret 99-100
  Mary 137 Nancy 87
  Priscilla 87 Robert
  87 Samuel 137
  Susan 129 Susanna
  88 T 171 Thomas 10
  20 26 36 42 50 76
  87-90 94 102 104
  117 126 129 134
  136-137 167 179-
  180 182 188 191
  194-196 198-199
  Thos G 166 William
  19 50 87-88 98 136
  160 180 192-193
  197
POLLOAK, 86
POLLOCK, 84 George
  147 John 87
  Magdalene 87
  Margarette 86 Robert
  86-87 W H 86
PORTER, Col 86-87
  Margarette 86

PRICE, Anne 121
PULLOAK, 84-86
QUEARY, John 124 168
　188 196 198 204
RAMSAY, 154 David
　104 Francis A 114 J
　G M 100 106 Mary
　134
RAMSEY, J G 98 J G M
　203
READ, William 27-28
　105
REAP, Peter 32
REESE, David 129-130
　168 188 198 Rev Dr
　184 Susan 129
　Thomas 104 132
RICHARDSON, Col 91
RITCHIE, 153 157
ROBINSON, John 145
　Robert 50 62 145
　196
ROSS, Lizzie 118
　Nicholas 118
ROWAN, President 147
ROWDON, Lord 96
RUPERT, 86
RUTHERFORD, 97 120
　136 138 Gen 109
　111 129
SCONNEL, Miss 115

SHARPE, Jemima 112
　Thomas 112
SHELBY, Miss 107
SHIPLEY, Edward 145
　George 145
SIMESON, John 50 197
　199
SMITH, Gov 147
　William 139
SPARKS, Jared 59
SPRATT, Susanna 88
　Thomas 88
SPRINGS, John 109
　Mary 109
STEDMAN, 95
STERLING, Lord 101
STEVENSON, Andrew
　58 60 J W 60 Mr 59
STINSON, D G 114
STOKES, Gov 18
SUMTER, 121 Gen 123
SWAIN, David L 30
TAIT, C 176 178
TASKER, Margarette 86
THESTON, George 145
　Hugh 145
THOMAS, 130
THOMPSON, Capt 143-
　144 James 145 John
　142
TICKNOR, Mr 155

INDEX

TONER, Dr 27
TRYON, 108 182 Gov 107 181
TUCKER, 58
TURNER, Mr 59
VANCE, 53 Gov 51
WADDELL, 108 Gen 107
WALLACE, J A 116
WALLIS, James 33-35 82 114
WASHINGTON, 182 Gen 27 92 180 President 109
WATSON, Elkanah 94 98
WELLING, J C 61 Rev Dr 57
WELLS, Samuel Adams 153
WESTON, Job 180
WHEELER, 20 26 30 Col 60 112 J H 93
WILHITE, James 204-205
WILLIAMSON, 19 24 Dr 153 157 Hugh 18 159 175 Mr 158
WILLSON, William 179
WILSON, Benjamin 35 Capt 119 David 118-119 Mary 137 Robert 118 Samuel 134 200 Violet 134 William 136 Zaccheus 117-118 Zacheus 188 196 Zacheus Sr 167
WINTHROP, 125
WIRT, 154 Mr 156 198
WITHERSPOON, Dr 104
YATES, Gen 93

www.ingramcontent.com/pod-product-compliance
Lightning Source LLC
Chambersburg PA
CBHW050147170426
43197CB00011B/1992